Growing Confident and Capable Kids

Practical Parenting Tools to Nurture Resilience, Initiative, and Emotional Strength in Children

Patty R. Adams

Table of Contents

Thank You for Reading!

I hope you found *Growing Confident and Capable Kids* helpful and enjoyable!

Your feedback is invaluable to me and helps others discover this book.

If you could take a moment to **leave a review**, I'd greatly appreciate it. Scan the QR code below to leave your review:

Thank you!

Patty

Visit the **Cantelune Press** website for more compassionate books that meet you where you are!

https://cantelunepress.com/

Introduction

In today's fast-paced world, we face a parenting paradox that challenges our deepest instincts. While we yearn to protect our children from every possible setback, we simultaneously recognize that their future success depends on developing resilience, critical thinking, and emotional intelligence. During my two decades of working with families and raising three children of my own, I've witnessed firsthand how this delicate balance shapes not just childhood experiences but lifelong capabilities.

The journey of raising emotionally capable children isn't just about managing feelings; it's about fostering independence, building decision-making skills, and developing the resilience needed for life's inevitable challenges. Consider Marcus, a tenth-grader who struggled with anxiety about his future career path. His parents, though well-intentioned, had always steered him toward 'safe' choices. When they learned to step back and create space for his exploration, Marcus discovered a passion for environmental science that transformed not just his academic performance but his entire outlook on life.

The truth is, our children's development of emotional intelligence, critical thinking, and resilience depends not on our constant intervention but on our ability to create opportunities for guided independence. Like teaching a child to ride a bike, we must know when to hold on and when to let go. This applies whether we're helping a toddler learn to self-soothe, supporting a grade-schooler in resolving peer conflicts, or guiding a teenager through complex life decisions.

Throughout this book, we'll explore practical strategies for fostering independence while maintaining strong emotional connections. You'll learn to identify opportunities for growth, understand the difference between protective and limiting behaviors, and develop tools for supporting your child's journey toward emotional maturity. We'll examine how these skills translate into real-world success, from academic achievement to career choices and relationships.

This isn't about stepping away from our children; it's about stepping into a new role as their emotional coach rather than their emotional manager. We'll explore how to create safe spaces for learning through experience, how to build strong emotional bonds while encouraging autonomy, and most importantly, how to trust both yourself and your child throughout this process.

Drawing from both professional experience and personal insights, I'll share stories of families who've successfully navigated this journey, along with practical tools and strategies you can implement immediately. Whether you're dealing with a preschooler's first social challenges or a teenager's career decisions, you'll discover how to support growth while avoiding the trap of overprotection.

Remember, your child's journey toward emotional competence and independence is not a straight line but a winding path filled with opportunities for learning and growth. Every challenge they face, every decision they make, and every consequence they experience contributes to their development of resilience and emotional intelligence. Our role isn't to eliminate these experiences but to provide the support and guidance that allows them to learn from them.

As we begin this exploration together, know that your concerns about finding the right balance are both normal and necessary. They reflect your deep commitment to your child's well-being. This book will serve as your guide, helping you navigate the complex territory between protection and independence, always with the goal of nurturing emotionally intelligent, resilient individuals capable of charting their own course in life.

Let's embark on this journey together, understanding that sometimes the most powerful gift we can give our children is the space to grow, learn, and occasionally stumble; all while knowing we're there to support, not rescue. The rewards of this approach, watching our children develop into confident, capable individuals ready to tackle life's challenges, make every moment of letting go worthwhile.

Chapter 1:

The Overprotection Trap: Why Stepping Back is the New Stepping Up

"It is not what you do for your children, but what you have taught them to do for themselves that will make them successful human beings."
— Ann Landers

Picture yourself teaching a child to ride a bike; there's that crucial moment when you have to let go of the seat, even though every instinct screams to keep holding on. This moment perfectly captures the essence of modern parenting: knowing when to protect and when to step back, a balance that has become increasingly challenging in our anxiety-driven world. This delicate dance between protection and independence shapes not just our children's present experiences but their future ability to navigate life's challenges with confidence and wisdom. As both a parent and a child development specialist, I've seen how this balance impacts everything from a child's decision-making abilities to their career choices later in life.

The journey of learning to step back often begins with small moments that feel monumental. Take Tony, a bright 10-year-old whose mother had always managed his homework schedule. When she first allowed him to handle his assignments independently, he struggled at first, missing deadlines and earning lower grades than usual. However, through this experience, he developed his own system for tracking tasks and learned to make decisions about prioritizing his work. These skills proved invaluable years later when he confidently tackled college applications and internship opportunities.

Our role as parents isn't just about protecting our children from immediate challenges; it's about equipping them with the tools they'll need throughout their lives. When we step back appropriately, we're not just teaching them to pack their own backpack or handle homework; we're helping them develop critical thinking skills, emotional resilience, and the confidence to face life's bigger decisions.

Consider how these early experiences of independence cascade into adult life. Children who learn to manage age-appropriate challenges grow into teenagers who can navigate complex social situations, and eventually into adults who can confidently pursue their chosen career paths and maintain healthy relationships. Each small victory in childhood, whether it's resolving a playground dispute or recovering from a forgotten assignment, builds the foundation for handling bigger life decisions.

The story of Emma and her forgotten gym clothes illustrates this beautifully. What might seem like a minor incident, borrowing from the lost and found instead of calling mom, actually represents a crucial moment in developing problem-solving skills and self-reliance. These are the same qualities that will help her face bigger challenges later in life, from choosing a college major to navigating workplace dynamics.

In our rapidly changing world, the ability to think critically, adapt to new situations, and bounce back from setbacks has become more valuable than ever. When we allow our children to experience age-appropriate challenges and natural consequences, we're not just helping them through today's difficulties; we're preparing them for a future where resilience and independent thinking are essential life skills.

This chapter will explore how to recognize these opportunities for growth, understand when to step back, and learn how to support our children's journey toward independence without abandoning our role as their safety net. We'll examine practical strategies for fostering resilience while maintaining strong emotional bonds, and discover how this approach creates not just capable children but confident, adaptable adults ready to forge their own path in life.

Understanding the Psychology of Overprotection: How Good Intentions Create Unintended Consequences

The path to overprotection often begins with love and the deepest desire to see our children thrive. As parents, we instinctively want to shield our children from pain, smooth their path, and ensure their success. However, this natural impulse, when taken too far, can paradoxically hinder their growth and development in profound ways.

Consider Maria's story, a mother who managed every aspect of her 12-year-old son's academic life. She would review his work nightly, email teachers about minor assignment details, and step in at the first sign of a grade slipping below an A. While her intentions were admirable, her son began showing signs of anxiety about performing tasks independently. When he reached high school, he struggled with basic decision-making, constantly seeking validation before making even simple choices about his coursework. This pattern followed him to college, where he had difficulty choosing a major and managing his own academic schedule.

The psychology behind overprotection reveals an intricate web of parental anxiety and societal pressures. When we constantly monitor and manage our children's experiences, we unknowingly send a powerful message: 'You can't handle this on your own.' This message becomes deeply internalized, shaping how children view their own capabilities and their place in the world.

Perhaps most concerning is how overprotection impacts critical thinking and decision-making skills. When children don't have opportunities to make age-appropriate decisions and experience their consequences, they miss crucial learning experiences that build confidence and judgment. Jenny, a high school senior I worked with, struggled with choosing a college major because she had never been allowed to make significant decisions independently. Her parents had always guided her course selections, extracurricular activities, and even her friend groups, leaving her unsure of her own preferences and abilities.

The impact extends into emotional regulation and resilience. Children who are consistently shielded from disappointment or failure often develop what psychologists call 'learned helplessness,' a belief that they cannot handle challenges without intervention. This mindset can persist into adulthood, affecting everything from career choices to relationships.

Consider how this plays out in professional settings. Young adults who weren't allowed to experience natural consequences in childhood often struggle with workplace dynamics. They may have difficulty handling criticism, solving problems independently, or adapting to new situations; all crucial skills in today's rapidly changing job market.

The antidote to overprotection isn't neglect or complete hands-off parenting; it's thoughtful, graduated independence. Take the case of David, whose parents consciously shifted their approach when he was thirteen. Instead of managing his homework schedule, they helped him develop his own system for tracking assignments. Yes, he missed some deadlines initially, but through these experiences, he learned time management and responsibility. By his senior year, David was confidently managing multiple AP courses and college applications, skills that served him well in his future career.

Building resilience requires exposure to manageable challenges and the opportunity to develop problem-solving skills. When we understand the psychology of overprotection, we can begin to identify areas where stepping back might actually be stepping up as parents. This might mean allowing our children to experience the natural consequences of forgotten homework, navigate social conflicts independently, or make decisions about their extracurricular activities.

The goal is to create what psychologists call a 'scaffolded independence,' providing support while gradually increasing autonomy. This approach helps children develop the emotional tools and decision-making abilities they'll need throughout their lives. It's about finding the sweet spot between protection and independence, where children can develop the resilience and confidence they'll need for future success.

Remember, our role as parents isn't to eliminate all challenges from our children's paths; it's to help them develop the skills to navigate those challenges successfully. When we understand how overprotection can inadvertently undermine this development, we can make more conscious choices about when to step in and when to step back, ultimately fostering the independence and resilience our children need for long-term success.

Recognizing the Signs: When Protection Becomes Overprotection

Like most parents, I often catch myself hovering near my children on the playground, ready to prevent any potential fall or conflict. This instinct to protect is natural, but recognizing when it crosses into overprotection requires honest self-reflection and awareness. Through my work with families, I've observed how subtle this line can be, yet how crucial it is to recognize.

Consider the case of eight-year-old Thomas, whose mother, Sarah, found herself completing portions of his science project late one night. While she justified it as helping him succeed, this pattern of intervention was actually undermining Thomas's ability to develop crucial planning and problem-solving skills. It wasn't until Thomas struggled with independent work in middle school that Sarah realized her 'help' had delayed his development of essential life skills.

The signs of overprotection often appear in everyday moments. When we constantly interrupt our children's play to offer unsolicited advice, regularly speak for them in social situations, or frequently remind them of obvious safety considerations, we're likely crossing that line. These behaviors, while well-intentioned, send a subtle message that we don't trust their judgment or capabilities.

Decision-making patterns offer another clear indicator. If your child seems paralyzed by simple choices or constantly seeks validation for basic decisions, this might reflect an environment where independent thinking hasn't been sufficiently encouraged. Lucy, a typically developing 12-year-old, struggled to choose her own clothes or decide what to eat for lunch; signs that her parents' well-meaning guidance had become excessive control.

Watch for signs in social interactions as well. When children show unusual reluctance to engage in age-appropriate social activities without parental presence, or when parents find themselves mediating every minor peer conflict, these are red flags. The goal isn't to abandon our children to difficult social situations, but to guide them in developing their own conflict resolution skills.

Academic involvement provides another window into potential overprotection. Are you checking the online grade portal multiple times daily? Do you email teachers about minor assignment details before your child has attempted to address issues themselves? These behaviors, while common, can hinder the development of academic independence and responsibility.

Physical independence offers clear indicators, too. If your child shows age-inappropriate dependency for basic tasks like packing their bag, making simple snacks, or getting dressed, it's worth examining whether overprotection might be limiting their growth. Remember Charlotte, whose 10-year-old still waited for her to lay out clothes each morning; a habit that had evolved from convenience into dependency.

The emotional impact of overprotection often manifests in anxiety about new experiences or excessive fear of failure. Children who have been overprotected may show unusual resistance to taking age-appropriate risks or trying new activities without extensive parental reassurance. This pattern can limit their ability to develop resilience and confidence in their own capabilities.

Career counselors increasingly report seeing young adults struggling with basic decision-making and problem-solving skills, often a long-term consequence of childhood overprotection. These individuals frequently have difficulty choosing career paths, handling workplace challenges, or advocating for themselves professionally. The roots of these struggles often trace back to childhoods where natural consequences and independent decision-making were limited.

Technology has added new dimensions to overprotection. The ability to constantly monitor our children's locations, communications, and academic progress can make it tempting to maintain unnecessary levels of oversight. While some monitoring is appropriate, excessive digital surveillance can undermine the development of personal responsibility and self-regulation.

Recognition of these signs doesn't mean we should suddenly withdraw all support. Instead, it offers an opportunity to gradually adjust our parenting approach, allowing our children to develop the skills they'll need for future success. This might mean letting them experience the natural consequences of forgotten homework, navigate peer relationships more independently, or take age-appropriate risks in their physical activities.

Remember, the goal isn't to eliminate protection entirely but to find the balance that allows for growth while maintaining safety. When we recognize signs of overprotection in our parenting, we can begin making conscious choices to step back, allowing our children to develop the confidence, resilience, and decision-making skills they'll need throughout their lives.

Building the Stepping Back Toolkit: Practical Strategies for Fostering Independence

Creating opportunities for independence requires more than just stepping back; it demands a thoughtful approach that builds both confidence and capability. Through my work with families, I've discovered that the most effective toolkit combines emotional support with practical strategies that evolve as children develop their decision-making abilities and critical thinking skills.

Consider the story of Maya, a hesitant 9-year-old whose parents began implementing a 'decision ladder' approach. They started with simple choices; what to pack for lunch or wear to school, before progressing to more complex decisions like managing homework schedules or resolving peer conflicts. Within months, Maya wasn't just making decisions more confidently; she was showing improved problem-solving skills across multiple areas of her life.

The foundation of effective independence-building lies in creating what I call 'safe zones for failure,' controlled environments where children can experience setbacks without devastating consequences. This might mean letting your child handle their morning routine independently, knowing they might be late once or twice, or allowing them to manage their allowance even if it means making spending mistakes. These experiences build not just practical skills but also emotional resilience.

Another powerful tool is the art of reflective questioning. Instead of providing immediate solutions, ask questions that promote critical thinking: 'What do you think might happen if...?' or 'How could you handle this differently next time?' When 11-year-old James struggled with a group project, his father resisted the urge to email the teacher. Instead, he helped James explore different approaches to working with his teammates, leading to valuable lessons in communication and collaboration.

The toolkit must also include strategies for building decision-making confidence. Start with the '3-Choice Method,' offering three viable options rather than unlimited choices or binary decisions. This provides enough freedom for meaningful choice while preventing decision paralysis. As children demonstrate good judgment, gradually expand their decision-making scope.

One often overlooked aspect of fostering independence is teaching children to recognize when they genuinely need help versus when they're seeking reassurance. Jess, a middle school teacher, shares how she helps students develop this discernment by having them try three solutions independently before asking for assistance. This simple strategy has helped countless children build problem-solving confidence while learning when it's appropriate to seek support.

Physical independence deserves special attention in our toolkit. Create age-appropriate checklists for daily tasks, gradually transferring responsibility from parent to child. Start with simple tasks like packing a school bag or making a bed, then progress to more complex responsibilities like managing a homework schedule or planning weekly activities. The key is consistency. Once you've transferred a responsibility, resist the urge to take it back when things don't go perfectly.

Learning to evaluate risks and make safety decisions is another crucial component. Rather than constant warnings about potential dangers, help children develop their own risk assessment skills. Ask them to identify possible hazards and brainstorm safety measures. This approach builds both independence and judgment, crucial skills they'll need throughout their lives.

The toolkit must also address emotional independence. Teach children to recognize and articulate their feelings, and help them develop their own coping strategies for difficult emotions. When 10-year-old Zoe felt overwhelmed by test anxiety, her mother helped her create a personal calming routine instead of simply trying to fix the situation. This empowered Zoe to manage her emotions independently.

Technology management represents a modern addition to our independence toolkit. Rather than implementing strict controls, work with children to develop healthy media habits and self-regulation skills. This might involve creating family guidelines together or helping them recognize when screen time is affecting their mood or productivity.

Remember that setbacks are not failures but opportunities for growth. When children stumble, whether it's a forgotten assignment or a mismanaged conflict, help them analyze what happened and plan for better outcomes next time. This approach transforms mistakes from sources of shame into valuable learning experiences.

Finally, celebrate progress in ways that reinforce independence rather than dependence. Instead of praising the outcome ('Great grade!'), acknowledge the process ('You really figured out a good way to study for that test'). This shifts the focus from external validation to internal satisfaction with their own capability and growth.

Building independence is a gradual process that requires patience, consistency, and trust in our children's abilities to learn and grow from experience. When we equip them with the right tools and support their journey with understanding rather than control, we help them develop not just independence, but the confidence and capability they'll need for lifelong success. As we close this first chapter, we've explored how the delicate balance between protection and independence shapes not just our children's present experiences but their future abilities to navigate life's challenges. Through stories like David developing his homework system and Jess finding solutions at school, we've seen how small moments of independence build the foundation for larger life skills.

The journey of stepping back isn't just about letting go; it's about fostering critical thinking, emotional resilience, and the confidence needed for life's bigger decisions. When children learn to handle age-appropriate challenges, from playground conflicts to forgotten assignments, they develop the problem-solving abilities and self-reliance that will serve them well into adulthood. These skills become invaluable as they face important life choices about education, careers, and relationships.

Perhaps most importantly, we've discovered that overprotection, despite its good intentions, can limit our children's development of essential life skills. By understanding when to step back and allowing natural consequences to become teaching moments, we create opportunities for genuine growth and learning. The confidence gained from successfully navigating these early challenges becomes the bedrock of future success.

As you move forward, remember that each small step back you take as a parent creates space for your child to step forward into their own capability. Whether it's letting them pack their own backpack, resolve their own conflicts, or face the consequences of forgotten homework, these moments build the resilience and decision-making skills they'll need throughout life. Trust that by understanding and implementing these principles, you're not just protecting your child; you're empowering them to develop the emotional tools they'll need for a lifetime of success.

In the chapters ahead, we'll explore specific strategies for different ages and situations, but for now, start small. Look for one opportunity each day to step back and trust your child's journey. Remember that every time you resist the urge to immediately fix your child's problems, you're giving them the gift of discovering their own strength and capability. This is how we raise not just independent children, but confident, resilient adults ready to forge their own paths in life.

Chapter 2:

Emotional Milestones: Your Child's Journey from Dependence to Independence

"To develop autonomy, children need to make choices and learn from the consequences—both positive and negative."
— *Dr. Ross Greene*

Every child's journey toward emotional independence follows a unique path, much like a butterfly emerging from its chrysalis; it cannot be rushed or forced, only supported and nurtured. As parents, our role isn't to cut open the chrysalis, but to create an environment where our children feel safe enough to spread their own wings. Just as every butterfly's emergence follows its own timeline, our children's emotional development unfolds at its unique pace, shaped by both innate characteristics and the environment we create. This journey of emotional growth encompasses far more than just managing feelings; it's about developing critical thinking, decision-making abilities, and the resilience needed for life's challenges.

Through my experiences working with families, I've observed that emotional milestones often prove more challenging for parents to navigate than physical ones. While we readily celebrate first steps and academic achievements, we sometimes overlook equally important emotional victories, like when our child first shows empathy toward others or independently resolves a conflict.

Consider Mike, a bright 10-year-old who struggled with project planning. His mother had always broken down his assignments into manageable steps, creating detailed schedules and reminders. When a major science project was assigned, instead of following her usual approach, she decided to step back. Mike initially felt overwhelmed, but gradually developed his own system for tackling the work. He experienced some setbacks, including a late-night scramble to finish, but ultimately created a project that was truly his own. The pride in his eyes when presenting wasn't just about the grade; it was about discovering his capability to manage complex tasks independently.

This transformation in Mike's approach to challenges reflects a broader truth about emotional development: when children learn to navigate difficulties on their own, they develop not just confidence but also crucial executive functioning skills that will serve them throughout their lives. These skills become particularly valuable as they approach adulthood, influencing everything from career choices to relationship management.

As we explore the journey from emotional dependence to independence, we'll examine how these foundational experiences shape future success. We'll look at how allowing children to face age-appropriate challenges builds the problem-solving abilities and resilience they'll need in college, their careers, and adult relationships. The skills developed through early experiences of managed independence, whether handling conflict with peers or learning to organize schoolwork, become the building blocks for adult decision-making and emotional regulation.

In this chapter, we'll break down key emotional milestones while providing practical tools for recognizing and supporting your child's progress. You'll learn to identify opportunities where stepping back allows your child to develop critical thinking skills and emotional resilience. We'll explore how these early experiences of independence create a foundation for future success, helping your child develop the confidence and capability to navigate increasingly complex life challenges.

Remember, supporting emotional development isn't about pushing our children toward independence before they're ready or holding them back when they're capable of more. It's about creating an environment where they can safely explore their capabilities while knowing we're there when truly needed. This balanced approach helps children develop the emotional intelligence, decision-making skills, and resilience they'll need to thrive in an increasingly complex world.

Understanding Age-Appropriate Emotional Independence: Key Milestones from Toddler to Teen

The path to emotional independence isn't a straight line but rather a series of expanding circles, each one reaching further into independence while maintaining a secure connection to family. Every stage brings unique opportunities for growth that shape not just emotional awareness but also critical thinking and decision-making abilities that will serve children throughout their lives.

In the earliest years (0-2), babies progress from complete dependence to their first tastes of emotional autonomy. During this foundational period, consistent emotional support creates the security needed for healthy exploration. When 18-month-old Becky reached for a toy just beyond her grasp, her father resisted the urge to immediately hand it to her. Instead, he stayed close, offering encouraging words as she problem-solved her way to success. These small moments of supported struggle lay the groundwork for future resilience.

The toddler years (2-3) bring the famous 'I do it myself' phase, a critical period for developing initiative and confidence. Three-year-old John insisted on putting on his own shoes, even though it made the morning routine longer. His parents learned to build in extra time, recognizing that these moments of independence were building his problem-solving skills and self-reliance. When he finally mastered the task, his pride showed how these early victories built the foundation for tackling bigger challenges.

Preschoolers (3-5) begin developing more sophisticated emotional awareness and social skills. This age brings opportunities for handling peer relationships and managing frustration. When four-year-old Sofia encountered conflicts during playdates, her mother stopped immediately intervening. Instead, she helped Sofia identify her feelings and brainstorm solutions, building both emotional vocabulary and conflict resolution skills that would serve her well in future relationships.

Middle childhood (6-12) opens up new frontiers for independence in both practical tasks and emotional challenges. This is when children begin developing the executive functioning skills crucial for future success. Ten-year-old Matt learned to manage his homework schedule independently, experiencing both the natural consequences of procrastination and the satisfaction of meeting deadlines through his own efforts. These experiences build not just responsibility, but also the time management skills essential for future academic and career success.

The teenage years (13-18) bring perhaps the most significant shift toward emotional independence. This stage requires parents to move from managers to consultants, available for guidance while allowing teens to take increasing ownership of their decisions. When sixteen-year-old Aimee struggled with friendship drama, her parents resisted the urge to intervene. Instead, they helped her examine her options and supported her as she navigated the situation independently, building crucial interpersonal skills she'll need in adult relationships.

Throughout these stages, children need opportunities to practice decision-making in age-appropriate ways. A toddler might choose between two outfit options, while a teenager manages their entire social calendar. These escalating levels of choice and responsibility build the critical thinking skills essential for adult life.

It's important to recognize that emotional independence develops alongside practical skills. When seven-year-old Noah learned to make his own breakfast, he gained more than just the ability to prepare food. He developed planning skills, learned to assess his own needs, and gained confidence in his ability to care for himself. These practical achievements reinforce emotional growth and independence.

The journey toward emotional independence also involves learning to regulate emotions and handle disappointment, skills crucial for future career success and personal relationships. When twelve-year-old Lily wasn't chosen for the school play, her parents acknowledged her disappointment while letting her work through the emotions independently. This experience helped her develop resilience and coping strategies she'll draw on throughout life.

Remember that progress often includes temporary setbacks. Children may show great emotional maturity one day and seem to regress the next, particularly during times of stress or transition. This is normal and expected. Our role as parents is to maintain consistent support while gradually expanding the scope of experiences we allow our children to navigate independently, always considering their individual temperament and developmental readiness.

Supporting emotional independence means creating opportunities for children to practice new skills while maintaining a safety net. It's about finding that sweet spot between challenge and support where true growth occurs. As children successfully navigate increasingly complex emotional and practical challenges, they develop not just independence but also the confidence and competence they'll need to thrive in adulthood.

Building Emotional Resilience Through Natural Consequences

Natural consequences offer our children authentic learning experiences that shape not just behavior, but also critical thinking and decision-making abilities. When we allow children to experience these teaching moments, within safe and age-appropriate boundaries, we help them develop the resilience and judgment they'll need throughout life's journey.

Consider twelve-year-old Alex, who consistently forgot his soccer equipment for after-school practice. His mother had always rushed home to bring his forgotten gear until we discussed letting natural consequences become the teacher. The first time Alex had to sit out practice and watch his teammates play, he experienced disappointment and frustration. However, this experience prompted him to create his own system for preparing gear the night before. More importantly, it sparked a realization that he could solve problems independently. This lesson extended beyond sports; Alex began applying this newfound organizational skill to homework and other responsibilities.

The power of natural consequences lies in their ability to teach multiple skills simultaneously. When seven-year-old Sally forgot her lunch, rather than having it delivered to school, she learned to problem-solve by getting lunch from the cafeteria. This experience taught her not just responsibility, but also how to handle unexpected situations, communicate her needs to adults, and manage disappointment. These skills form the foundation for future workplace and relationship success.

The scope of learning through natural consequences expands as children grow. For teenagers, missing a homework deadline might mean a lower grade, while poor money management results in having no funds for weekend activities. These experiences, though temporarily uncomfortable, help develop the judgment and foresight crucial for adult decision-making. When sixteen-year-old Tammy overspent her monthly allowance, instead of providing extra money, her parents allowed her to experience the natural outcome of her choices. This led to her developing budgeting skills she'll use throughout life.

However, implementing natural consequences effectively requires careful discernment. Safety always comes first; we never allow natural consequences that could cause serious harm or trauma. A child forgetting their jacket on a cool spring day provides a valuable learning opportunity; the same scenario in freezing winter weather requires parental intervention. The key lies in distinguishing between situations that offer growth opportunities and those requiring protection.

Creating an environment where mistakes are viewed as learning opportunities rather than failures proves crucial. When ten-year-old Chris forgot his musical instrument on performance day, rather than rushing to bring it, his parents helped him process the experience afterward. They asked questions like 'What did you learn from this?' and 'How might you handle this differently next time?' This approach helps children develop problem-solving skills while maintaining emotional security.

Natural consequences also play a vital role in developing future career readiness. When children learn to link their choices with outcomes early in life, they develop the cause-and-effect thinking essential for professional success. For instance, when fourteen-year-old Anne had to handle the consequences of submitting a rushed project, she learned valuable lessons about time management and quality of work that will serve her well in future academic and professional endeavors.

To effectively implement natural consequences, focus on maintaining emotional support while stepping back from fixing the situation. After a natural consequence occurs, help children reflect with questions that promote critical thinking: 'What happened because of your choice?' 'What other options did you have?' 'What might you do differently next time?' This reflection process helps children internalize lessons and develop better decision-making skills.

Remember that emotional resilience develops gradually, with each natural consequence offering an opportunity for growth. Sometimes, children need to experience the same consequence multiple times before the lesson fully resonates. This isn't a sign of failure but a normal part of the learning process. Each experience builds upon previous ones, gradually developing the emotional intelligence and problem-solving abilities needed for life success.

By allowing our children to experience age-appropriate natural consequences within a supportive environment, we help them develop not just resilience but also critical thinking, decision-making skills, and emotional intelligence. These experiences create a foundation of capability and confidence that will serve them well as they navigate increasingly complex life challenges, from college applications to career choices and beyond.

The Parents' Role: Balancing Support with Space for Growth

Finding the sweet spot between supporting your child and allowing space for growth feels like walking a tightrope; lean too far in either direction, and you risk undermining their development. Through years of working with families, I've discovered that this balance isn't about finding a fixed point, but rather about developing a dynamic approach that evolves with your child's capabilities and challenges.

Consider Abigail, a typically reserved 9-year-old who dreamed of joining the school debate club. Her mother's instinct was to sign her up, prepare her arguments, and coach her through every meeting. Instead, we discussed letting Abigail take the lead while remaining available for support. Abigail gathered the courage to sign herself up, struggled through her first few debates, and gradually developed her own speaking style. When she won her first debate, her victory wasn't just about public speaking; it was about discovering her own strength through supported independence.

The key lies in recognizing when to step forward and when to step back. Think of yourself as a spotter in rock climbing, present and alert, but not actually climbing for your child. Your role is to ensure safety while allowing them to experience the challenge, build strength, and occasionally stumble on their path to mastery.

This approach becomes particularly crucial as children approach adolescence and begin making decisions that impact their future.

When 14-year-old Craig struggled with choosing his high school electives, his father resisted the urge to simply tell him what to take. Instead, he helped Craig explore his interests and consider long-term implications, guiding him through the decision-making process while letting Craig own the final choice. This experience built not just decision-making skills, but also the confidence to tackle bigger life choices ahead.

Creating opportunities for supported independence requires thoughtful preparation. Rather than jumping in to solve problems, try asking questions that promote critical thinking: 'What do you think might work?' 'What could happen if you try that?' 'What's your backup plan?' These questions help children develop problem-solving skills while knowing they have your support.

Sometimes, the hardest part is managing our own anxiety as parents. When seven-year-old Dawn wanted to walk to her friend's house alone for the first time, her mother's instinct was to say no. Instead, they worked together to create a safety plan, practiced the route, and established check-in protocols. This collaborative approach helped both mother and daughter navigate the transition to greater independence.

The role of emotional support evolves as children grow. For younger children, it might mean being physically present while they tackle new challenges. For older kids, it often means being available for consultation while letting them take the lead in problem-solving. When 16-year-old Steven faced conflict with his coach, his parents resisted the urge to intervene. Instead, they helped him analyze the situation and supported his decision to have a direct conversation with the coach, an experience that built both confidence and communication skills.

Your support should also extend to celebrating effort and resilience, not just success. When 11-year-old Kelly struggled with a difficult math concept, her parents acknowledged her persistence rather than focusing solely on grades. This approach helps children develop a growth mindset that will serve them well in facing future challenges.

Remember that stepping back doesn't mean disappearing - it means being present differently. Create regular check-in times where children can share concerns and seek guidance. This routine helps them feel supported while learning to manage daily challenges independently. It also provides opportunities to assess whether your current balance of support and space aligns with your child's developing capabilities.

As your child grows, actively look for opportunities to transfer responsibility in age-appropriate ways. Start with small tasks and gradually increase complexity. When children show mastery in one area, identify the next growth opportunity. This progressive approach builds confidence while maintaining security.

The ultimate goal isn't perfect independence; it's developing capable, confident individuals who know how to seek and use support effectively. Success means raising children who can navigate challenges, make thoughtful decisions, and know when to ask for help. This balance of support and space creates resilient adults who can handle life's complexities while maintaining healthy relationships with others.

Your role as a parent in this journey is to be the secure base from which your child can safely explore and grow. By maintaining emotional availability while allowing age-appropriate independence, you help your child develop the confidence, competence, and critical thinking skills they'll need throughout life. This approach not only supports their current development but also lays the foundation for future success in relationships, career, and personal growth. As we conclude our exploration of emotional milestones, remember that supporting your child's journey to independence isn't just about managing emotions; it's about fostering the critical thinking, decision-making abilities, and resilience they'll need throughout life. Like the gradual emergence of a butterfly from its chrysalis, this development cannot be rushed, only supported with patience and understanding.

Throughout this chapter, we've seen how emotional independence develops alongside practical capabilities, from Mike learning to manage his science project to Sofia navigating playground dynamics. These experiences build far more than just emotional awareness; they create the foundation for future success in college, careers, and relationships.

The journey from emotional dependence to independence brings opportunities at every stage. Whether it's a toddler's first 'I do it myself' moment or a teenager's complex social decisions, each step builds crucial life skills. We've explored how natural consequences serve as powerful teachers, building not just responsibility but also the critical thinking and problem-solving abilities essential for adult life.

Your role in this journey evolves as your child grows, from primary emotional regulator to trusted consultant. The key lies in maintaining emotional availability while gradually expanding the space for independent decision-making and problem-solving. Remember that stepping back doesn't mean stepping away. It means being present differently, creating opportunities for growth while maintaining a secure foundation.

As you move forward, consider these essential principles:

- Trust your child's capacity for growth while maintaining appropriate safety boundaries
- Allow natural consequences to teach valuable lessons when appropriate
- Create opportunities for age-appropriate decision-making and problem-solving
- Celebrate effort and resilience, not just success
- Remember that progress includes temporary setbacks

Most importantly, recognize that every emotional milestone your child achieves strengthens not just their independence but also their capacity for future success. The child who learns to navigate peer conflicts independently develops skills for future workplace relationships. The teenager who manages their own schedule builds time management abilities crucial for college and career.

In the next chapter, we'll explore how natural consequences can become powerful teachers in your child's journey toward emotional maturity. Until then, remember that your child's path to emotional independence, like every butterfly's emergence, follows its own perfect timeline. Your role isn't to force that timeline but to create an environment where growth can unfold naturally and confidently.

Trust that each small step toward emotional independence, whether it's solving a playground dispute or managing a project deadline, builds the foundation for your child's future success. By balancing support with space for growth, you're not just raising an emotionally competent child; you're nurturing the resilient, capable adult they will become.

Chapter 3:

The Power of Natural Consequences: Building Resilience Through Real Experience

"Behind every behavior is a feeling. And behind every feeling is a need. When we meet that need rather than focus on the behavior, we begin to deal with the cause, not the symptom."
— *Ashleigh Warner*

The most profound lessons in life rarely come from lectures or warnings; they come from experiencing the natural outcomes of our choices. As parents, our instinct to protect our children from discomfort often robs them of these valuable learning opportunities that build emotional resilience and practical wisdom. Through experiencing natural consequences, children develop decision-making muscles that will serve them well into adulthood. These early lessons in managing everyday challenges lay the foundation for critical thinking skills essential for success in careers, relationships, and life's major decisions. When children learn to navigate setbacks and solve problems independently, they gain confidence in their abilities and develop resilience that carries them through future challenges.

Consider Michael, a high school student who learned valuable lessons about responsibility in his early years through natural consequences. His parents had allowed him to experience the results of forgetting assignments or missing deadlines, always within safe boundaries. These experiences taught him to anticipate outcomes, plan ahead, and take ownership of his responsibilities. Now, as he prepares for college, Michael demonstrates remarkable self-reliance and problem-solving abilities that his peers, who were constantly rescued by their parents, often lack.

The impact of natural consequences extends far beyond immediate behavior changes. When children experience the direct results of their choices, they develop an internal framework for decision-making that proves invaluable in adulthood. From career choices to financial management, these early lessons in cause and effect help shape thoughtful, resilient adults capable of navigating life's complexities with confidence.

Think of natural consequences as life's built-in teaching tools, offering lessons that no lecture or warning could match. When a child forgets their jacket and feels cold, they learn more about personal responsibility than they would from a dozen reminders. When they miss an activity because they didn't complete their tasks on time, they gain firsthand experience in time management and priority setting, skills crucial for future academic and professional success.

The process of allowing natural consequences requires parents to develop their own emotional resilience. It's not easy to watch our children experience discomfort or disappointment, but understanding that these moments are valuable learning opportunities helps us maintain perspective. By stepping back appropriately, we demonstrate our confidence in our children's ability to learn and grow from their experiences.

Understanding Natural vs. Logical Consequences: A Framework for Growth

Natural consequences offer children authentic life lessons that shape their decision-making abilities and emotional growth. When a child forgets their homework, the natural result is facing their teacher unprepared and experiencing disappointment. These moments, though uncomfortable, create direct connections between choices and outcomes that prepare children for adult responsibilities and relationships.

The power of natural consequences lies in their authenticity. A teenager who oversleeps and misses an important event learns time management more effectively than through any parental lecture. These experiences shape neural pathways that inform future decisions about responsibility, from managing college coursework to meeting workplace deadlines. The discomfort of natural consequences also builds emotional resilience, a crucial skill for navigating life's inevitable challenges.

However, not every situation calls for natural consequences. When safety is at risk or when the impact would unfairly affect others, logical consequences become our teaching tools. These thoughtfully designed outcomes should maintain three key qualities: they should be Related to the behavior, Respectful in delivery, and Reasonable in scope. For example, if a child repeatedly misuses art supplies, temporarily losing access to those materials teaches responsibility while maintaining safety.

The framework for implementing logical consequences requires careful consideration of your child's developmental stage and the specific situation. A preschooler who throws toys might lose access to those specific items for a short period, while a teenager who breaks curfew might face reduced social privileges. The key is maintaining consistency while adjusting the scope as children develop greater capability for independent decision-making.

Picture Aleah, a middle school student who consistently procrastinated on long-term projects. Rather than micromanaging her work or allowing the natural consequence of failing grades, her parents implemented a logical consequence system. Each week, Aleah needed to show progress on her projects to maintain her regular weekend social activities. This approach helped her develop time management skills while preserving her academic standing; a balance between learning and protection.

Creating space for both natural and logical consequences nurtures critical thinking and problem-solving abilities. Children learn to anticipate potential outcomes, weigh options, and make informed decisions; skills that become increasingly valuable as they navigate career choices, relationships, and financial decisions in adulthood. A child who learns through age-appropriate consequences develops confidence in their ability to handle challenges independently.

When implementing consequences, maintain a supportive presence while allowing the teaching moment to unfold. Express empathy for any disappointment while standing firm in the face of the consequences. This balance shows children that we care about their feelings while trusting their ability to learn and grow from experience. Remember, our goal isn't punishment but rather guiding children toward greater emotional intelligence and self-regulation.

The long-term benefits of experiencing appropriate consequences extend far beyond immediate behavior changes. Children develop an internal compass for decision-making, building resilience and confidence that serves them throughout their lives. These early lessons in cause and effect help shape thoughtful, capable adults who can navigate life's complexities with wisdom and self-assurance.

Age-Appropriate Risk-Taking: When to Step Back and Let Experience Teach

Every child's journey toward independence requires carefully calibrated opportunities to take age-appropriate risks. These moments of controlled challenge build the foundation for resilience, critical thinking, and sound judgment that serve them throughout life. Understanding when to step back requires recognizing the difference between productive discomfort that leads to growth and unnecessary risks that could cause lasting harm.

For young children, appropriate risks might mean climbing playground equipment independently while a parent watches from a distance, or attempting to tie their shoes even when it takes longer than having help. These seemingly small moments of independence lay the crucial groundwork for bigger challenges ahead. Consider six-year-old Mark, who initially feared the monkey bars at his local playground. His father resisted the urge to lift him across, instead staying close while Mark built up the courage to try himself. After several attempts and minor slips, Mark mastered the crossing; his face beaming with pride not just at the accomplishment, but at overcoming his fear.

As children enter elementary school, risk-taking evolves to include social and academic challenges. Let them handle peer conflicts when possible, manage their homework responsibilities, and face the natural consequences of forgotten assignments or mismanaged time. These experiences develop problem-solving skills that become invaluable in high school, college, and eventually the workplace. A missed assignment today might mean a lower grade, but the lesson learned prevents missed deadlines in future careers.

For teenagers, appropriate risks expand to include greater independence in decision-making about time management, social relationships, and personal responsibilities. When fifteen-year-old Suzy wanted to take on a part-time job, her parents helped her think through the implications for her schedule rather than making the decision for her. This allowed Suzy to develop critical thinking skills about balancing priorities, an essential skill for adult life.

The key to supporting healthy risk-taking lies in creating an environment where children feel secure enough to step out of their comfort zone. This means maintaining a calm, supportive presence while resisting the urge to immediately solve problems or prevent all discomfort. When children know they have a safe base to return to, they're more likely to take the calculated risks that lead to growth.

Consider risk-taking as a muscle that needs regular exercise to grow stronger. Without opportunities to practice decision-making in situations with moderate stakes, children struggle to develop good judgment for handling bigger challenges later in life. A child who never learns to manage their homework schedule independently may struggle with project management in their future career. Someone who never navigates social conflicts without parental intervention might find workplace relationships particularly challenging.

Parents can support healthy risk-taking by:

- Creating opportunities for graduated independence
- Maintaining presence without immediate intervention
- Discussing potential outcomes before challenges arise
- Reflecting on experiences afterward to reinforce learning
- Celebrating effort and resilience, not just success

This approach helps children develop what psychologists call 'internal locus of control' – the belief that they can influence outcomes through their own actions. A child who learns to assess risks and make decisions develops confidence in their judgment, leading to better decision-making about everything from peer relationships to career choices.

The long-term benefits of appropriate risk-taking extend far beyond childhood. Adults who learned to handle age-appropriate challenges in their youth typically show greater resilience in facing career obstacles, maintaining healthy relationships, and navigating life's inevitable setbacks. They develop a realistic understanding of their capabilities and limitations, leading to better judgment in both personal and professional contexts.

Remember that stepping back doesn't mean stepping away; it means being fully present while allowing children to experience the natural consequences of their choices within safe boundaries. This strategic approach to parenting requires trust in both the process and your child's innate capacity for growth. When children experience age-appropriate risks within a supportive framework, they develop the emotional tools and decision-making abilities needed to navigate life's challenges successfully.

Supporting Without Rescuing: Building Emotional Resilience Through Natural Learning

Supporting a child's journey toward independence requires a delicate balance between being present and allowing space for growth through experience. This balance shapes not just immediate behavior but builds the foundation for lifelong resilience, decision-making capabilities, and emotional intelligence that serve children well into their adult lives and careers.

Consider the story of Andy, a fourth-grader who struggled with project management. Rather than stepping in to organize his science fair project, his mother Patricia helped him break down the task into manageable pieces and create his own timeline. When he fell behind schedule, she resisted the urge to take over. Instead, she asked guiding questions that helped him think through solutions. The night before the fair, Andy stayed up later than usual to finish, a natural consequence that taught him more about time management than any lecture could have. This experience not only improved his approach to future projects but also developed critical thinking skills that would later help him excel in his first job.

Supporting without rescuing means being emotionally present while allowing children to navigate challenges within their capabilities. When twelve-year-old Maisie forgot her basketball uniform for an important game, her father's instinct was to rush home to get it. Instead, he helped her think through options: she could borrow from a teammate, talk to her coach about sitting out, or find another solution. Maisie ultimately borrowed shorts from a friend and learned valuable lessons about responsibility and problem-solving that extended far beyond sports.

The key lies in distinguishing between supporting and solving. Support might mean helping a child identify possible solutions, discussing potential outcomes, or offering emotional encouragement through challenges. Solving, on the other hand, removes the opportunity for growth by handling the situation for them. When we consistently solve our children's problems, we inadvertently communicate that we don't trust their abilities to handle challenges.

Consider how this approach builds crucial workplace skills. A child who learns to manage homework deadlines independently is better prepared for project management in their career. Someone who practices resolving peer conflicts in elementary school develops communication skills that serve them in future professional relationships. These early experiences create neural pathways for problem-solving that become invaluable in adult life.

The process requires parents to develop their own emotional resilience. Watching our children struggle with challenges can trigger anxiety and an overwhelming urge to step in. However, maintaining a calm, supportive presence while allowing them to work through difficulties helps children build confidence in their problem-solving abilities. This confidence becomes particularly important as they face bigger decisions about college, careers, and relationships.

Creating a framework for supported independence involves:

- Establishing clear expectations about responsibilities
- Providing tools and strategies rather than solutions
- Maintaining emotional availability without taking over
- Celebrating effort and learning from mistakes
- Gradually increasing independence as capabilities grow

Remember that support looks different at various developmental stages. For a young child, it might mean standing nearby as they navigate playground equipment. For a teenager, it could involve discussing options for handling a difficult social situation without directing their choice. The goal remains consistent: building capability and confidence through guided experience.

Each time we resist the urge to rescue, we create an opportunity for growth. When six-year-old Joshua struggled to zip his coat, his teacher's patience in letting him work through frustration paid off in both immediate skill development and longer-term persistence. These small moments accumulate to build a strong foundation of self-reliance and problem-solving ability.

The long-term impact of this approach extends into adult decision-making. Children who learn to handle age-appropriate challenges develop better judgment about everything from personal relationships to career choices. They enter adulthood with a robust toolkit for navigating life's inevitable obstacles and a deep confidence in their ability to handle whatever comes their way.

Supporting without rescuing ultimately prepares children for the realities of adult life, where success often depends on resilience, adaptability, and independent problem-solving. By allowing children to experience and learn from manageable challenges within a supportive framework, we help them develop the emotional and practical skills needed for lifelong success. As we conclude our exploration of natural consequences and their role in developing emotional resilience, remember that the path to building capable, confident adults often runs through moments of productive struggle. The lessons learned through experiencing natural outcomes shape not just immediate behavior, but forge the critical thinking and decision-making abilities essential for success in relationships, careers, and life's greater journey.

Through this chapter, we've seen how allowing children to experience age-appropriate consequences creates powerful learning opportunities that no amount of lecturing could match. From playground problem-solving to homework management, these experiences build the neural pathways for sound judgment and emotional resilience. The confidence gained through successfully navigating challenges becomes part of their emotional DNA, informing choices far into adulthood.

Consider Maisie's transformation after being allowed to solve her forgotten basketball uniform situation. Not only did she develop immediate problem-solving skills, but she gained confidence that carried over into other areas of her life. These moments of supported independence create ripple effects, building capabilities that serve children well beyond childhood, from managing college coursework to navigating workplace relationships.

As you move forward in your parenting journey, remember that stepping back isn't about disengagement; it's about strategic support that allows natural learning to unfold. When your child faces a challenge within their capabilities, pause before jumping in to rescue them. Ask yourself: Will protecting them from this discomfort serve their long-term development? Often, the most loving action is maintaining a supportive presence while allowing them to work through challenges independently.

The key principles we've explored through this chapter extend far beyond childhood:

- Natural consequences provide authentic learning experiences that shape future decision-making
- Age-appropriate challenges build problem-solving skills essential for adult success
- Supporting without rescuing develops confidence and resilience
- Early experiences with managing consequences create foundations for career and life choices
- Building emotional resilience requires opportunities to face and overcome challenges

As we look ahead to the next chapter on building your child's emotional toolkit, carry forward this understanding: Every time you resist the urge to rescue your child from a manageable challenge, you're helping them develop the emotional muscles they'll need for life's bigger adventures. Trust in their capacity for growth, maintain your supportive presence, and remember that today's small struggles are building tomorrow's capable, confident adults.

Chapter 4:

Your Child's Emotional Toolkit: Age-Appropriate Skills for Life's Challenges

"Don't do for a child what they can do for themselves."
— *Maria Montessori*

Every child comes into this world with the capacity for emotional growth, but it's through carefully calibrated challenges and support that they develop their emotional toolkit. Like a master craftsperson selecting the right tools for each project, parents must understand which emotional skills are appropriate for their child's developmental stage and how to nurture these abilities effectively. Just as a carpenter carefully selects the right tools for each project, we as parents must thoughtfully build our children's emotional, decision-making, and problem-solving capabilities. The journey from childhood to adulthood requires developing a comprehensive set of life skills that will serve them not just in managing emotions, but in navigating career choices, relationships, and life's inevitable challenges.

Consider Teresa, a bright 12-year-old who struggled with test anxiety. Rather than immediately seeking accommodations or intervening with teachers, her parents helped her develop strategies to manage stress and prepare effectively. Through trial and error, Teresa discovered that breaking study sessions into smaller chunks and using breathing techniques helped her stay focused. These skills later proved invaluable when she faced college interviews and job applications, demonstrating how early emotional tools translate into lifelong capabilities.

The emotional toolkit we help our children develop extends far beyond managing feelings; it encompasses critical thinking, resilience, and the ability to make sound decisions independently. When children learn to process setbacks and challenges healthily, they're building neural pathways that will serve them throughout their lives. The confidence gained from solving problems independently in elementary school becomes the foundation for tackling bigger challenges in high school, college, and eventually their chosen career paths.

This holistic approach to emotional development acknowledges that success in adult life requires more than just academic achievement or emotional awareness. It demands the ability to think critically, bounce back from setbacks, and navigate complex social situations. When we allow children to experience age-appropriate challenges and support them in finding their own solutions, we're not just helping them manage today's homework or friendship struggles; we're preparing them for future leadership roles, career transitions, and life's unexpected turns.

As we explore the essential tools for your child's emotional growth in this chapter, we'll focus on practical strategies that build not just emotional intelligence but also decision-making skills and resilience. We'll examine how these capabilities interweave to create a strong foundation for future success, whether your child dreams of becoming an entrepreneur, artist, or scientist. Most importantly, we'll look at how stepping back at the right moments allows these crucial skills to develop naturally, creating confident, capable individuals ready to navigate their own path forward.

Building Age-Appropriate Emotional Regulation Skills: From Toddler Tantrums to Teen Stress Management

Emotional regulation develops like climbing a ladder; each rung represents new skills and capabilities that build upon earlier foundations. The journey begins in toddlerhood with raw, unfiltered emotions and progresses through increasingly sophisticated strategies for managing life's challenges. Understanding this progression helps us provide appropriate support without overstepping.

Take Finlay, age three, who would melt down every time his block tower toppled. His mother resisted the urge to prevent the towers from falling or to immediately rebuild them herself. Instead, she acknowledged his frustration while introducing simple coping tools: 'I see you're angry. Should we take three big dragon breaths together?' Over time, Finlay began using these breathing techniques independently, laying the groundwork for more advanced emotional regulation.

By elementary school, children are ready for more nuanced emotional tools. Consider Isabella, age eight, who initially panicked over every math test. Rather than requesting special accommodations or studying with her for hours, her parents helped her develop a 'calm-down toolkit,' including positive self-talk, break-taking strategies, and preparation routines she could implement herself. These skills proved valuable not just for tests but for handling various challenges throughout her academic career.

The preteen years bring unique emotional regulation challenges as social dynamics become more complex. Twelve-year-old Neil struggled with gaming-related anger until his parents helped him create his own cool-down system. Instead of banning video games or constantly monitoring his reactions, they guided him in recognizing his triggers and developing personal strategies for managing frustration. This self-awareness and ability to self-regulate later helped him handle high-pressure situations in competitive sports and academic competitions.

Teenagers face perhaps the most complex emotional landscape, navigating academic pressures, social media, and future planning. For seventeen-year-old Angie, college application stress manifested in sleepless nights and anxiety attacks. Rather than taking over the process, her parents helped her break down the overwhelming task into manageable pieces while teaching mindfulness techniques. This approach not only helped with immediate stress but equipped her with valuable tools for managing future career and life transitions.

The key to supporting emotional regulation at any age lies in recognizing the difference between scaffolding and rescuing. When seven-year-old Tobias felt overwhelmed by a science project, his father resisted the urge to simplify or complete portions of the work. Instead, they discussed how to break the project into smaller tasks and identified specific times when Tobias could ask for help. This experience taught Tobias not just about science, but about project management and emotional resilience.

Critical thinking and decision-making skills develop alongside emotional regulation. Consider Belinda, age thirteen, who struggled with social media anxiety. Instead of implementing strict controls or monitoring her accounts, her parents engaged her in discussions about digital boundaries and helped her develop her own guidelines for healthy social media use. This approach fostered both emotional regulation and critical thinking about technology use, skills that served her well in navigating future professional online presence.

As children progress through these stages, our role shifts from active emotion coach to supportive consultant. This transition requires trust in our children's developing capabilities while remaining emotionally available. The goal isn't to eliminate emotional challenges but to equip our children with tools to handle them effectively, preparing them for independent adult life where they'll need to manage workplace stress, relationship dynamics, and career decisions.

Remember that setbacks in emotional regulation aren't failures; they're opportunities for growth and learning. When ten-year-old Ethan lost his spot on the soccer team, his initial reaction was intense disappointment and anger. His parents allowed him space to feel these emotions while guiding him through reflection and problem-solving. This experience helped him develop resilience and adaptability, traits that would prove invaluable in future academic and professional challenges.

The ultimate measure of success in emotional regulation isn't the absence of strong feelings or challenges, but the ability to navigate them effectively while maintaining focus on long-term goals. These skills become particularly crucial as young adults enter the workforce, manage professional relationships, and make important life decisions. By supporting age-appropriate emotional regulation development, we're not just helping our children manage today's challenges; we're preparing them for a lifetime of emotional intelligence and resilience.

Problem-Solving Strategies That Grow With Your Child: Teaching Independent Decision-Making

Teaching independent decision-making isn't just about helping children solve today's problems; it's about equipping them with a lifelong approach to facing challenges with confidence and creativity. As children develop these skills, they build the foundation for future success in careers, relationships, and personal growth.

Consider ten-year-old Dan, who struggled with organizing his homework schedule. Instead of creating a rigid system for him, his mother guided him through exploring different approaches. They discussed his learning style, energy patterns throughout the day, and extracurricular commitments. Through trial and error, Dan developed his own method; completing harder subjects right after school when his mind was fresh and saving creative projects for evening. This experience taught him not just time management, but also the valuable process of analyzing problems and testing solutions.

The journey of developing problem-solving abilities follows a natural progression that mirrors cognitive development. For preschoolers, decision-making often starts with simple choices: 'Would you like to wear the red shoes or the blue shoes?' These early experiences build confidence in making choices and understanding their outcomes. Carlie, age four, began making her own breakfast choices between three healthy options. Sometimes her combinations were unusual, carrots with yogurt, but experiencing these natural consequences helped her refine her decision-making process.

As children enter elementary school, they're ready for more complex problem-solving strategies. Katie, age eight, faced a common friendship challenge when her best friend started playing with someone else at recess. Instead of intervening, her father helped her brainstorm different approaches to the situation. Katie decided to suggest inclusive games that all three could play together. This solution not only resolved the immediate issue but also taught her valuable lessons about compromise and creative problem-solving.

The preteen years bring opportunities for more sophisticated decision-making tools. Fourteen-year-old Henry wanted to join both the band team and basketball program, but worried about managing his time. His parents resisted the urge to make the decision for him and instead helped him gather information about each activity's requirements. They guided him through creating a pros and cons list and considering long-term implications. Henry ultimately chose the band team, having reached this decision through careful analysis rather than parental direction.

Technology can present unique problem-solving challenges. When sixteen-year-old Claire struggled with social media distractions during homework, her parents avoided imposing strict rules. Instead, they encouraged her to analyze the issue and develop her own solution. Claire created a system of timed study blocks with short social media breaks, teaching her valuable lessons about self-regulation and productivity that she later applied in college.

Critical thinking becomes increasingly important as children approach adulthood. Rather than providing ready answers, guide them through analyzing situations from multiple angles. When seventeen-year-old Jason considered different college majors, his parents helped him research career paths, interview professionals in various fields, and evaluate his own strengths and interests. This process equipped him with decision-making skills that proved valuable throughout his career.

Real-world experience often provides the best teaching moments. Fifteen-year-old Aisha wanted to start a small jewelry-making business. Instead of handling the logistics for her, her parents encouraged her to research local craft fairs, calculate costs, and develop a marketing plan. While some aspects of her business didn't work as planned, these challenges provided valuable lessons in entrepreneurship and resilience.

The goal isn't to eliminate struggles but to help children develop systematic approaches to handling challenges. When twelve-year-old Tyler faced a group project with uncooperative teammates, his parents helped him break down the problem into manageable parts: What was within his control? What resources could he access? What were possible solutions and their likely outcomes? This analytical approach became a template he could apply to future challenges.

Remember that effective problem-solving skills develop gradually and require practice. Create safe opportunities for children to make decisions and experience consequences. Allow them to struggle with age-appropriate challenges while providing emotional support and guidance. These experiences build not just problem-solving abilities but also confidence, resilience, and independence; essential qualities for success in any future endeavor.

Developing Emotional Resilience Through Guided Challenges and Natural Consequences

Building emotional resilience requires more than just theoretical knowledge; it demands practical experience navigating life's challenges within a supportive framework. Just as muscles grow stronger through strategic exercise, emotional resilience develops through carefully calibrated exposure to age-appropriate challenges and the natural consequences that follow our choices.

Consider twelve-year-old Ben, who consistently forgot his baseball equipment for after-school practice. Rather than rushing home to retrieve the forgotten gear, his parents helped him explore the natural consequences of his actions. Missing practice due to forgotten equipment taught Ben more about responsibility than any lecture could have. Within a month, he developed his own system for preparing his gear the night before, a habit that later served him well in managing college coursework and professional responsibilities.

The journey to emotional resilience parallels the development of critical thinking and decision-making abilities. When nine-year-old Cathy struggled with a challenging history project, her mother resisted the urge to simplify the task or provide solutions. Instead, they discussed different approaches, with Cathy making the final decisions about her project strategy. Though some attempts failed, each setback strengthened her problem-solving skills and built confidence in her ability to overcome obstacles.

Natural consequences provide powerful learning opportunities when handled appropriately. For instance, when fourteen-year-old Peter chose to spend his allowance immediately rather than save for a desired gaming console, experiencing the disappointment of delayed gratification taught him valuable lessons about financial planning and patience. These early experiences with money management laid the groundwork for more complex financial decisions in adulthood.

Creating opportunities for guided independence allows children to develop their own coping strategies. Take Zara, age ten, who felt anxious about public speaking. Instead of requesting she be excused from class presentations, her parents helped her develop techniques to manage her anxiety. She learned to practice in front of stuffed animals, use deep breathing exercises, and visualize success. These tools not only helped with presentations but also became part of her broader emotional regulation toolkit.

The development of resilience extends beyond handling immediate challenges to building long-term capabilities. Sixteen-year-old Ana faced repeated rejections while applying for summer internships. Rather than having her parents make calls on her behalf, she learned to refine her approach, improve her interview skills, and persist despite disappointment. This experience proved invaluable when she later navigated the competitive job market after college.

Critical to building resilience is understanding that struggle itself has value. When eleven-year-old Jim joined the robotics club with no prior experience, he initially felt overwhelmed by the technical challenges. His parents encouraged him to view difficulties as learning opportunities rather than failures. This mindset shift not only helped him persist in robotics but also approach future challenges in high school and college with greater confidence.

Age-appropriate challenges should stretch comfort zones while maintaining safety. For example, allowing ten-year-old Briony to plan and cook a family meal involved real responsibility with manageable risks. While her first attempts weren't perfect, the experience taught valuable lessons about planning, problem-solving, and recovering from mistakes. These skills translated well to other areas of responsibility as she grew older.

Decision-making capabilities strengthen alongside emotional resilience. When thirteen-year-old Diego struggled to balance schoolwork with soccer practice, his parents guided him through analyzing his priorities and time management rather than making decisions for him. This process helped him develop both practical skills and emotional tools for handling future life balancing acts.

The path to resilience isn't always smooth, but this is precisely what makes it valuable. Consider fifteen-year-old Mia, who initially panicked when group projects went awry. Through guided experience handling team dynamics and project setbacks, she developed stronger leadership skills and emotional regulation strategies. These capabilities later proved essential in her college studies and early career roles.

Remember that building resilience is a gradual process that requires both challenge and support. The goal isn't to eliminate difficulties but to help children develop the confidence and capabilities to handle life's inevitable ups and downs. Through this journey, they build not just emotional resilience but also the critical thinking, decision-making, and problem-solving skills essential for success in any future endeavor. As we conclude our exploration of your child's emotional toolkit, let's reflect on the transformative power of building these essential life skills. Throughout this chapter, we've seen how emotional tools combine with critical thinking, decision-making abilities, and resilience to create a foundation for lifelong success. The stories of children like Tobias, Angie, and Cathy remind us that these capabilities don't emerge fully formed; they develop through carefully supported experiences and thoughtfully managed challenges.

The journey of building your child's emotional toolkit extends far beyond managing daily feelings and conflicts. It's about equipping them with the skills they'll need to navigate career choices, handle professional relationships, and make important life decisions. When we help children develop these tools early, we're not just addressing today's challenges; we're investing in their future capacity to handle everything from job interviews to workplace dynamics.

Remember the key principles we've explored: emotional regulation skills progress naturally from simple breathing exercises to complex stress management strategies. Problem-solving abilities grow through guided experience rather than direct intervention. Critical thinking develops when children have space to analyze situations and test solutions. Most importantly, resilience emerges when children face and overcome challenges within a supportive environment.

As you move forward, focus on creating opportunities for your child to build their emotional toolkit through real-world experience. Start small, let your toddler work through frustration with that challenging puzzle, allow your elementary schooler to navigate peer conflicts before stepping in, or give your teenager space to manage their own schedule and responsibilities. These moments of supported independence become the building blocks of emotional competence and future success.

Implementation might mean watching your child struggle momentarily with a difficult task or emotion. Remember that these struggles, when appropriately supported, aren't setbacks; they're valuable opportunities for growth that build the foundation for adult capabilities. Your role isn't to eliminate challenges but to provide the guidance and emotional support that allows your child to develop their own solutions.

Trust in this process of emotional development, knowing that each small step builds toward greater capabilities. When your child learns to manage homework stress today, they're building skills that will help them handle future career pressures. When they navigate friendship challenges independently, they're developing social intelligence that will serve them in professional relationships.

In the next chapter, we'll explore how to recognize when to step in and when to let go, building on the emotional toolkit we've developed here. Until then, remember that every time you resist the urge to immediately fix things for your child, you're giving them the gift of developing crucial life skills that will serve them well into adulthood.

You've got this, parents. Keep supporting, keep growing, and keep trusting in your child's journey toward emotional competence and independence. The toolkit you help them build today will become the foundation of their future success.

Chapter 5:

The Fine Line: When to Step In and When to Let Go

"Our job as parents is not to protect our children from every failure, but to prepare them to recover and grow because of it."
— *Jessica Lahey, The Gift of Failure*

The moment your child faces a challenge, your instinct as a parent is to rush in and solve the problem, but that instinct, while natural, isn't always what serves them best. Learning to distinguish between necessary intervention and valuable learning opportunities is perhaps one of the most crucial skills we can develop as parents. This delicate dance of intervention and independence shapes not just our children's present experiences but also their future capacity for resilience, critical thinking, and emotional intelligence. Each time we resist the urge to immediately step in, we create space for our children to develop the problem-solving skills and confidence they'll need throughout their lives, from navigating career choices to building meaningful relationships.

The journey toward finding this balance often begins with understanding our own parental instincts. When we constantly intervene in our children's challenges, we unknowingly send a message that undermines their confidence; we're telling them we don't trust their ability to handle life's obstacles. This pattern manifests in subtle ways: the teenager who struggles with basic decision-making because they've never had to exercise that muscle, or the young adult who feels paralyzed when facing career choices without parental guidance.

Consider how these early patterns of independence shape a child's future. A child who learns to navigate age-appropriate challenges develops not just immediate problem-solving skills but also the metacognitive abilities needed for future success. They learn to trust their judgment, evaluate risks, and develop the resilience needed for life's inevitable setbacks. Whether pursuing entrepreneurial ventures, managing workplace dynamics, or building lasting relationships, these foundational skills become invaluable assets.

I've witnessed countless examples of how this philosophy transforms both parent and child. Take Eleanor, a single mother who struggled to let her 10-year-old son Clement handle his own school project timelines. When Alex forgot about a science fair project until the night before, Eleanor's instinct was to stay up late helping him complete it. Instead, she helped him email his teacher, explaining his oversight and requesting an extension. This experience taught Clement valuable lessons about time management and taking responsibility for his actions. More importantly, it showed him that his mother trusted him to handle the consequences of his choices.

In this chapter, we'll explore practical strategies for discerning when to intervene and when to step aside. You'll learn to identify genuine risk situations versus growth opportunities, manage your own anxiety about stepping back, and create age-appropriate boundaries that support your child's development. Through understanding these principles, you'll discover that some of your child's most significant progress happens not when you step in, but when you step back with trust and intention.

Recognizing True Risk vs. Growth Opportunities: A Decision Framework

The ability to distinguish between true risks and growth opportunities fundamentally shapes your child's journey toward independence and resilience. True risks pose genuine threats to your child's safety or well-being, while growth opportunities, though sometimes uncomfortable, offer valuable chances for development and learning.

Consider fourteen-year-old Gary, who wanted to take the city bus alone to his after-school activities. His mother, Alexandra, initially felt tremendous anxiety about this request. Instead of making an immediate decision based on fear, she evaluated the situation systematically: Gary had demonstrated good judgment in other situations, understood safety protocols, and had practiced the route with her several times. The neighborhood was generally safe, and the bus route was straightforward. While there were genuine considerations to address, none presented unmanageable risks. The opportunity for Gary to develop independence, time management skills, and confidence outweighed the manageable risks involved.

When evaluating situations, focus on these key factors:

- Current Capabilities: Has your child demonstrated the necessary judgment and skills for the task?

- Environmental Context: What specific risks exist in the situation, and are they manageable?
- Growth Potential: What valuable skills or experiences could your child gain?
- Recovery Impact: If things don't go as planned, are the consequences manageable?

The framework extends beyond immediate safety considerations to long-term development. Take sixteen-year-old Chloe, who wanted to start an online jewelry business. Her parents recognized both risks (online safety, time management, financial responsibility) and opportunities (entrepreneurship, creative expression, business skills). Instead of shutting down the idea or taking control, they helped Chloe create safety protocols and business guidelines while letting her manage the venture independently. This experience became invaluable when she later pursued business studies in college.

Remember that risk assessment changes with age and individual development. What might be a true risk for an eight-year-old could be a perfect growth opportunity for a twelve-year-old. Even siblings of the same age may be ready for different levels of independence based on their individual maturity and experience.

Creating what I call 'challenge zones' helps children develop judgment in low-risk situations. For a six-year-old, this might mean ordering their own meal at a restaurant. For a teenager, it could involve planning a family day trip, including budget management and logistics. These scenarios provide safe spaces for developing critical thinking and decision-making skills that transfer to more significant life choices.

The most challenging aspect often isn't identifying risks but managing our own parental anxiety about stepping back. When ten-year-old Daniel wanted to walk to his friend's house alone, his father Jon felt intense anxiety. Through our sessions, Jon learned to distinguish between his emotional response and objective risk assessment. The walk involved crossing one residential street with a crossing guard; a manageable challenge that offered Daniel an opportunity to develop independence and street safety awareness.

This framework also helps parents maintain perspective during emotional moments. When seven-year-old Lily struggled with a challenging math problem, her mother, Rachel, felt compelled to provide the answer to ease Lily's frustration. By applying our decision framework, Rachel recognized this as a growth opportunity rather than a risk situation. Lily's struggle, though uncomfortable, was developing crucial problem-solving skills and resilience.

The goal isn't to eliminate all risks; that's neither possible nor desirable. Instead, aim to create an environment where your child can encounter and navigate age-appropriate challenges while developing the judgment they'll need for future decisions. Whether choosing a college, pursuing a career path, or navigating relationships, these early experiences in risk assessment and decision-making become invaluable reference points.

Think of yourself as a guide rather than a protector. Your role isn't to clear every obstacle but to help your child develop the tools to navigate challenges independently. This approach builds not just capability, but confidence; the kind that comes from knowing you can handle difficult situations because you've successfully done so before.

Managing Parental Anxiety While Stepping Back

As parents, letting go is perhaps one of the most challenging aspects of supporting our children's growth toward independence. That familiar knot in your stomach when your child faces difficulty isn't just normal; it's a sign of how deeply you care. However, learning to manage this anxiety effectively becomes crucial not just for your own well-being but for your child's development of resilience and self-reliance.

Consider the case of Dexter, whose daughter Karen was starting middle school. David found himself checking Karen's online grades multiple times daily and texting her throughout the school day. During our work together, he realized his anxiety was actually undermining Karen's confidence and ability to develop crucial academic independence. Through deliberate practice in stepping back, Dexter learned to check grades weekly instead of daily, allowing Karen to experience both the natural consequences of procrastination and the satisfaction of managing her own academic responsibilities.

Understanding the roots of parental anxiety often reveals deeper insights. Sometimes it stems from our own childhood experiences; perhaps times when we felt unsupported or overwhelmed. Other times, it's driven by societal pressures about 'perfect parenting' or comparing ourselves to other parents. Recognizing these underlying factors helps us separate our own emotional needs from our children's growth requirements.

Creating what I call 'anxiety pause points,' moments where you consciously evaluate whether your desire to intervene comes from necessary protection or anxiety-driven control, can transform your parenting approach. Ask yourself: Is this a true risk requiring my intervention, or am I stepping in to manage my own discomfort? This simple practice helps build your 'stepping back muscle' while ensuring interventions are thoughtful rather than reactive.

The journey to managing parental anxiety isn't about eliminating worry entirely; it's about developing a healthier relationship with it. Start by identifying specific triggers. Does academic performance cause more anxiety than social situations? Do physical activities trigger stronger protective instincts than emotional challenges? Understanding these patterns helps you develop targeted strategies for managing them.

Building your own support network becomes crucial in this process. Connect with other parents who share your commitment to fostering independence. Their experiences and encouragement can provide valuable perspective when your own anxiety threatens to overwhelm your better judgment. Remember, it's okay to feel anxious; it's how you manage that anxiety that matters.

Transform your role from manager to mentor by focusing on being emotionally present while resisting the urge to fix everything. When your child faces a challenge, try asking 'What do you think might work here?' rather than immediately offering solutions. This approach helps build their problem-solving skills while maintaining your supportive presence.

Celebrate the moments when stepping back leads to growth. Document these successes, both yours and your child's. When sixteen-year-old Rob successfully navigated his first job interview after practicing with you, handling the actual interview alone, that became a powerful reminder of the benefits of managing your anxiety and trusting your child's capabilities.

As you work through this process, remember that managing parental anxiety isn't just about your child's independence; it's about their future ability to navigate life's challenges confidently. Every time you successfully manage your anxiety and step back, you're teaching your child valuable lessons about emotional regulation, resilience, and self-trust.

Consider how this approach impacts your child's future. A young adult who has experienced supported independence is better equipped to handle college challenges, career decisions, and personal relationships. They develop not just practical skills but also the emotional intelligence to navigate life's uncertainties with confidence.

The most valuable gift we can give our children isn't protection from all difficulties; it's the confidence that comes from knowing they can handle challenges while we support them from a healthy distance. Your anxiety doesn't make you a bad parent; learning to manage it while supporting your child's independence makes you a more effective one.

Age-Appropriate Independence: Creating Safe Boundaries for Learning

The path to independence resembles learning to swim - you start in the shallow end with support, gradually moving into deeper waters as skills and confidence grow. Creating effective boundaries for learning means establishing flexible frameworks that expand naturally with your child's demonstrated capabilities and judgment.

Consider twelve-year-old Dion, who showed interest in cooking. His parents created a graduated system of kitchen privileges tied to demonstrated responsibility. He started with simple sandwich-making using only non-sharp utensils, progressed to supervised stovetop cooking, and eventually earned the right to prepare full meals independently. Each new privilege came with clear guidelines about safety, cleanup, and timing. This systematic approach built not just practical skills, but also critical thinking and risk assessment abilities that serve him well beyond the kitchen.

The key to effective boundaries lies in their adaptability and purpose. Rather than acting as rigid restrictions, well-designed boundaries serve as scaffolding for growth. Take fifteen-year-old Melanie's journey with time management. Instead of imposing strict schedules, her parents established core principles: homework completion before leisure activities, maintaining reasonable sleep hours, and meeting family commitments. Within these guidelines, Melanie developed her own system for balancing academics, social life, and personal interests; valuable skills she later applied to college and career planning.

Independence develops through progressive challenges within safe parameters. When eight-year-old Trisha expressed interest in managing her own school materials, her parents created a structured transition plan. They started with a simple checklist for packing her backpack, gradually expanded to homework planning, and eventually included project management. The occasional forgotten assignment became a natural learning opportunity rather than a crisis requiring parental intervention.

The impact of thoughtful boundaries extends far beyond childhood. Consider Aiden, now a successful software developer, who credits his early experiences with structured independence for his current problem-solving approach. His parents allowed him to explore computer programming within clear guidelines about screen time and online safety. This balanced freedom helped develop both technical skills and responsible technology use, crucial abilities in his chosen career.

Creating effective learning boundaries requires understanding your child's unique capabilities and challenges. Fourteen-year-old Graham struggled with impulsive decisions, so his parents designed boundaries that encouraged pause and reflection. Before making significant choices, Graham learned to consider key questions: What are the potential consequences? Have I thought through alternatives? This framework helped develop critical thinking skills essential for adult decision-making.

The art of boundary-setting lies in balancing protection with opportunity. When establishing independence zones, consider these essential elements:

- Clear communication of expectations and consequences
- Flexibility to adjust based on demonstrated responsibility
- Opportunities for guided decision-making
- Regular review and expansion of privileges
- Focus on building specific life skills

Remember that boundaries serve multiple purposes; they provide security while creating opportunities for growth. When thirteen-year-old Peggy wanted more social media freedom, her parents established guidelines that taught digital literacy and online safety while allowing appropriate social connection. These boundaries helped Peggy develop media awareness and responsible online behavior, skills crucial for modern professional and personal life.

Effective boundaries also teach children to recognize and respect limits in various contexts. This understanding becomes invaluable in professional settings, relationships, and personal goal-setting. Consider how early experiences with managed independence shape future career choices and work habits. A child who learns to work within structured freedom often becomes an adult who can balance autonomy and accountability effectively.

The ultimate goal isn't to control behavior but to develop judgment. When ten-year-old Tim wanted to spend his savings on an expensive toy, his parents used their money management boundaries as a teaching opportunity. Instead of simply saying no, they helped him analyze the purchase decision, considering alternatives and long-term value. This approach developed financial literacy skills that serve him well in adult life.

Creating safe boundaries for learning means recognizing that mistakes within these boundaries are valuable teachers. When children experience natural consequences in a supported environment, they develop resilience and problem-solving skills. These experiences become reference points for future challenges, whether navigating college life, career decisions, or personal relationships.

As you establish and adjust learning boundaries, focus on building transferable skills rather than just managing current behavior. The independence developed through well-structured boundaries creates a foundation for lifelong learning and adaptation. Your role isn't to eliminate all risks but to create an environment where age-appropriate challenges become opportunities for growth and development. As we conclude our exploration of when to step in and when to step back, remember that this journey of finding balance shapes not just your child's present experiences but their lifelong capacity for independence, critical thinking, and emotional resilience. The skills developed through carefully managed independence become the foundation for future success in careers, relationships, and life's inevitable challenges.

Think of your evolving role as a parent like that of a master rock climbing instructor. Initially, you're holding tight to the safety rope, providing constant support and guidance. But as your climber gains confidence and skill, you gradually give more slack, allowing them to navigate challenging sections independently while remaining present and alert. Your presence provides security, but their growth comes from facing and overcoming obstacles themselves.

The real power of balanced intervention lies in the message it sends to your child: 'I trust your capabilities, and I'm here to support you.' When Kerry, a mother in one of my workshops, stopped immediately solving her teen's friendship conflicts and instead became a sounding board for brainstorming solutions, she noticed her daughter not only handled social challenges more effectively but also began approaching other life decisions with greater confidence and thoughtfulness.

As you move forward, remember these key principles: distinguish between true risks and growth opportunities, manage your own anxiety about stepping back, and create age-appropriate boundaries that expand with your child's demonstrated capabilities. Success isn't measured by how many challenges you help your child avoid, but by how well you prepare them to handle life's inevitable obstacles.

In our next chapter, we'll explore how to create supportive environments that encourage emotional growth while maintaining healthy boundaries. Until then, practice the art of strategic stepping back. Each time you resist the urge to immediately intervene, you're helping your child build the problem-solving muscles they'll need for future success. Trust that your presence, even from a slight distance, provides the security your child needs to spread their wings and soar.

Your child's journey toward independence may have its ups and downs, but with thoughtful guidance and trust in their capabilities, they'll develop the confidence and resilience needed to navigate life's challenges successfully. Remember, the goal isn't to make their path smooth; it's to equip them with the tools they need to navigate any terrain they encounter, today and in their future.

Chapter 6:

Creating Safe Spaces: How to Support Without Smothering

"Adolescence is not about letting go. It's about hanging on during a very bumpy ride."
— Ron Taffel

The art of creating emotional safety for our children isn't about building impenetrable walls; it's about installing windows and doors that allow them to view and explore the world while knowing they have a secure base to return to. As parents, our instinct to protect can sometimes overshadow our children's need to experience and process emotions independently, but finding the right balance is crucial for their emotional development. This delicate balance becomes especially vital as we guide our children through their journey of self-discovery and emotional growth. Creating supportive environments means understanding that true emotional safety isn't about shielding children from all discomfort, but rather equipping them with the tools to navigate life's challenges with confidence and resilience.

Think of emotional safety like tending a garden; we provide the right conditions for growth while allowing nature to take its course. Just as a gardener knows when to prune and when to let plants strengthen against the wind, parents must develop the wisdom to recognize when stepping back actually provides the best support. This approach not only fosters emotional resilience but also builds the critical thinking and decision-making skills essential for success in adulthood.

When working with families, I've observed how creating these nurturing spaces requires an evolving approach that adapts to each child's unique developmental journey. Consider Caleb, a 12-year-old whose parents sought guidance when his anxiety about academic performance began affecting his sleep. Rather than immediately intervening with teachers or implementing strict study schedules, we worked on creating a 'safe zone' where Caleb could express his concerns without fear of judgment. His parents learned to listen without rushing to fix things, helping Caleb develop his own strategies for managing academic pressure.

The real breakthrough came when Caleb decided to approach his math teacher independently about his struggling grades. His parents remained supportive but allowed him to handle the situation himself. This experience not only improved his academic performance but also significantly boosted his confidence in problem-solving and self-advocacy skills that will serve him well in college and his future career.

As we explore this chapter, we'll examine practical ways to create these emotional safe spaces that encourage independence while maintaining supportive boundaries. We'll look at how to recognize when our protective instincts might be limiting our children's growth opportunities and how to adjust our approach to better support their emotional development. Most importantly, we'll learn strategies for maintaining that crucial balance between being emotionally available and allowing the independence necessary for developing resilience, critical thinking, and self-confidence; essential qualities for navigating both personal and professional challenges in adulthood.

Building Trust Through Emotional Availability: The Foundation of Safe Spaces

Creating emotional availability isn't just about being physically present; it's about fostering an environment where children feel genuinely seen, heard, and understood in their emotional journey. When we establish this foundation of trust, we empower our children to explore their emotions confidently while developing the critical thinking and decision-making skills they'll need throughout life.

Consider Heather, whose daughter Lucy struggled with making decisions about extracurricular activities. Instead of choosing for Lucy or pushing her toward specific options, Heather created space for exploration. She listened to Lucy's thoughts without judgment, asked open-ended questions about her interests, and supported her through the process of weighing different choices. When Lucy eventually chose drama club over soccer, despite Heather's personal preference for sports, Heather's supportive response strengthened their bond and Lucy's trust in her own decision-making abilities.

The key elements of emotional availability create opportunities for growth while maintaining healthy boundaries:

- Being present without hovering
- Acknowledging emotions without rushing to fix them
- Creating space for independent problem-solving
- Maintaining open dialogue about challenges and triumphs

- Supporting decisions while allowing natural consequences

This foundation becomes particularly crucial as children navigate increasingly complex social and academic challenges. Take fourteen-year-old Richard, who was struggling with friendship dynamics in high school. His father resisted the urge to contact other parents or school administrators, instead providing a safe space for Richard to process his feelings and brainstorm solutions. This approach not only helped Richard develop stronger social skills but also built his confidence in handling future interpersonal challenges.

Emotional availability evolves as children grow, requiring different approaches at different stages. For younger children, it might mean sitting nearby as they work through frustration with a puzzle, offering encouragement without taking over. For teenagers, it could involve being accessible for conversation while respecting their increasing need for emotional privacy and independence.

Being emotionally available doesn't mean being perfect; it means being authentic and consistent. When Sean's mother lost her temper during a particularly stressful morning, she later acknowledged her reaction and discussed better ways they both could handle similar situations. This honest communication actually strengthened their relationship and taught Sean valuable lessons about emotional regulation and responsibility.

Remember that emotional availability is about creating a foundation for lifelong skills. When children know they have a secure base to return to, they're more likely to take healthy risks, develop resilience, and build the critical thinking abilities essential for future success.

These skills translate directly into their adult lives, helping them navigate career challenges, relationships, and personal growth with confidence.

The true measure of emotional availability shows in unexpected moments. Like when Sonya's daughter independently handled a difficult situation with a teacher, then came home to share, not because she needed help, but because she knew her mother would celebrate her growth. These moments of connection and trust build the emotional intelligence and decision-making capabilities that serve children well into adulthood.

Creating this foundation requires balancing protection with autonomy. It means staying connected while gradually expanding the space for independent emotional processing. When we achieve this balance, we give our children the gift of emotional competence, an essential tool for personal and professional success throughout their lives.

Setting Healthy Boundaries: When Support Becomes Suffocation

The journey of raising emotionally intelligent children requires us to master a delicate art: knowing when to step in and when to step back. Like a dance between parent and child, the rhythm of support must adapt as our children grow, allowing enough space for them to develop their own emotional choreography while remaining close enough to catch them if they truly stumble.

Consider the story of Jeremy, a bright 13-year-old whose mother found herself constantly intervening in his academic life. She checked his assignments nightly, emailed teachers weekly, and managed his study schedule meticulously. While her intentions were admirable, Jeremy began showing signs of increased anxiety about school and diminishing confidence in his abilities. During our work together, we identified how this well-meant support was actually suffocating his development of essential life skills like time management, self-advocacy, and resilience.

The transformation began when his mother started gradually releasing control. She created a simple system where Jeremy took increasing responsibility for his schoolwork, while she remained available for consultation rather than direction. The initial weeks were challenging - Jeremy missed some assignments and received lower grades than usual. However, these natural consequences proved invaluable, teaching him more about responsibility than years of maternal micromanagement ever could.

Key signs that support may be crossing into suffocation include:

- Handling tasks your child is developmentally capable of managing
- Feeling anxious when not in control of your child's activities
- Regularly intervening in your child's social or academic challenges before they attempt solutions
- Making decisions that your child could reasonably make themselves
- Protecting your child from age-appropriate natural consequences

The impact of boundary issues extends far beyond childhood. When we consistently solve problems for our children, we inadvertently send a message that we don't trust their capabilities. This can lead to decreased confidence in decision-making, reduced resilience in facing challenges, and difficulties with independent problem-solving skills crucial for success in higher education and future careers.

Consider Liz, a talented high school junior whose father obsessively managed her college application process. Despite good intentions, his overinvolvement left Liz questioning her own judgment and feeling increasingly anxious about her future. Through establishing healthier boundaries, Liz took ownership of her college search, developing crucial skills in research, decision-making, and self-advocacy that served her well beyond the application process.

Setting healthy boundaries doesn't mean withdrawing support; rather, it means transforming how we offer that support. Instead of solving problems for our children, we can guide them through the problem-solving process. Instead of protecting them from every potential disappointment, we can help them develop strategies to cope with and learn from setbacks.

The process of establishing healthy boundaries often requires parents to manage their own anxiety about stepping back. It's natural to worry when we see our children struggle, but remember that these struggles, when age-appropriate and within safe limits, build the emotional muscles needed for lifelong resilience and success.

Think of boundaries like the edges of a playground; they provide a safe space for exploration while preventing truly dangerous situations.

Within these boundaries, children can test their limits, learn from mistakes, and develop confidence in their abilities. This approach nurtures not just emotional intelligence but also the critical thinking and decision-making skills essential for navigating adult life.

The most powerful moments often come when we resist the urge to intervene. Like when Jarret's English project didn't turn out as planned, and instead of jumping in to fix it, his mother helped him process his disappointment and brainstorm improvements for next time. These experiences build the emotional toolkit children need to handle future challenges, whether in relationships, careers, or personal growth.

Healthy boundaries create space for children to develop their own identity and confidence while knowing they have a secure base of support. This balance helps them build the self-reliance and emotional intelligence they'll need throughout their lives, especially as they navigate higher education, career choices, and adult relationships.

Creating Growth Opportunities: Balancing Protection with Independence

The path to emotional maturity and independence requires carefully crafted opportunities for growth, moments where children can stretch their capabilities while knowing they have support if truly needed. Like teaching a child to ride a bike, we must find that sweet spot between holding on and letting go, where learning and confidence-building naturally occur.

Consider the story of Ruby, a ten-year-old who wanted to start a small craft business selling friendship bracelets at the local farmers' market.

Rather than immediately jumping in to manage the project, her parents helped her outline the steps involved and let her take the lead. Ruby learned to calculate costs, organize materials, and handle customer interactions independently. When she struggled with pricing her items correctly the first week, her parents resisted solving the problem for her. Instead, they helped her review her sales and expenses, guiding her to discover solutions herself. This experience not only taught her practical business skills but also built confidence in her decision-making abilities.

Creating growth opportunities means carefully considering your child's current capabilities and stretching them just beyond their comfort zone. This 'zone of proximal development' is where the most powerful learning occurs. For instance, when eight-year-old Luke expressed interest in cooking, his parents started by teaching basic kitchen safety, then gradually increased his responsibilities from helping with simple tasks to preparing entire portions of family meals independently.

The key is to identify opportunities that challenge without overwhelming. Molly, a middle school student, wanted to attend a summer camp but was nervous about being away from home. Instead of immediately saying no or pushing her to attend the full session, her parents helped her start with a weekend program. This stepping-stone approach allowed Molly to build confidence gradually while developing essential independence skills.

Growth opportunities often present themselves in everyday situations:

- Allowing children to order their own meals at restaurants

- Having them plan and pack their own school lunches
- Letting them manage their homework schedule with guided oversight
- Encouraging them to resolve peer conflicts before stepping in
- Supporting them in planning and executing their own projects

These experiences build more than just practical skills; they develop critical thinking, decision-making abilities, and emotional resilience that serve children well into adulthood. When twelve-year-old Enzo faced a challenging group project at school, his parents resisted the urge to email the teacher about team dynamics. Instead, they helped him brainstorm communication strategies, allowing him to navigate the situation himself. This experience proved invaluable when he later faced similar challenges in his first job.

It's important to recognize that creating growth opportunities doesn't mean abandoning our children to sink or swim. Rather, it means being thoughtfully selective about when and how we intervene. Like a safety net beneath a trapeze artist, we're there if truly needed, but our presence shouldn't prevent the performance.

Consider how these early experiences shape future capabilities. When Ella struggled with managing her first bank account, the lessons learned from earlier experiences with allowance management helped her adapt and develop better financial habits. These building blocks of independence create a foundation for handling increasingly complex life challenges.

Remember that growth opportunities should evolve with your child's development. What works for a six-year-old won't necessarily suit a teenager. The key is maintaining that delicate balance between challenge and support, always considering how each experience contributes to their journey toward becoming capable, confident adults.

By thoughtfully creating these opportunities while maintaining appropriate safety nets, we help our children develop the resilience, problem-solving skills, and confidence they need for future success. This approach nurtures not just independence but also emotional intelligence and critical thinking abilities essential for navigating both personal and professional challenges in adulthood. As we conclude our exploration of creating safe spaces for emotional growth, we recognize that the true art of supportive parenting lies not in constructing perfect environments but in building resilient children who can navigate life's challenges with confidence. Throughout this chapter, we've seen how stepping back while remaining emotionally present creates powerful opportunities for children to develop crucial life skills that serve them well into adulthood.

The stories we've shared, from Caleb finding his voice with teachers to Molly going to Summer camp independently, demonstrate that emotional safety isn't about eliminating challenges; it's about providing the secure foundation from which children can explore, struggle, and ultimately triumph. These experiences build not just emotional resilience but also the critical thinking and decision-making capabilities essential for future success in both personal and professional realms.

Creating safe spaces for emotional growth requires us to balance several key elements:

- Maintaining emotional availability without hovering
- Setting boundaries that evolve with our children's capabilities
- Providing opportunities for supported independence
- Building trust through consistent support
- Allowing natural consequences while ensuring basic safety
- Fostering critical thinking and problem-solving skills

As you move forward in your parenting journey, remember that each step back you take, while remaining emotionally present, creates space for your child's confidence to grow. Whether it's letting them navigate social challenges, manage their responsibilities, or make age-appropriate decisions, these moments of supported independence become the building blocks of their emotional resilience and future success.

Most importantly, creating safe spaces isn't about perfection; it's about progress. Your role isn't to prevent every fall or solve every problem, but to provide that crucial combination of support and space that allows your child to develop their own emotional strength. By mastering this balance, you're not just nurturing their emotional well-being today; you're equipping them with the tools they'll need to thrive in relationships, careers, and life's various challenges tomorrow.

The journey of creating safe spaces for emotional growth is ongoing, evolving as your child develops and faces new challenges. Trust that by maintaining this delicate balance between support and independence, you're giving your child one of the most valuable gifts possible: the confidence to navigate their own path while knowing they have a secure base to return to whenever needed.

Chapter 7:

The Connection Paradox: Building Bonds Through Independence

"Emotional intelligence begins to develop in the earliest years. All the small exchanges children have with their parents, teachers, and with each other carry emotional messages."
— *Daniel Goleman*

The strongest roots grow not from constant handling, but from the perfect balance of support and space to expand. As parents, our deepest instinct is to hold our children close, yet the most profound connections often develop when we master the art of stepping back. This balance between closeness and independence shapes not just our children's present development, but their future success in relationships, careers, and life decisions. Through my years of working with families, I've seen how children who learn to navigate challenges with supported independence develop stronger decision-making abilities and emotional resilience that serve them well into adulthood.

Consider Jamie, a teenager I worked with recently, whose early experiences with supported independence transformed her approach to career planning. While her peers relied heavily on their parents to chart their course, Jamie showed remarkable initiative in researching colleges and potential careers. She attributed this confidence to her parents' long-standing practice of letting her make age-appropriate decisions, starting from elementary school. Whether it was choosing extracurricular activities or managing her study schedule, each small decision helped build the critical thinking skills she now uses to shape her future.

The connection between early independence and adult success becomes particularly evident in how children approach challenges. Those who learn to trust their judgment while knowing support is available tend to become more adaptable professionals and more resilient individuals. They're more likely to take calculated risks, innovate in their chosen fields, and bounce back from setbacks; all crucial skills in today's rapidly changing world.

This approach to parenting, offering support while fostering independence, creates what I call the 'resilience ripple effect.' Each time a child successfully navigates a challenge independently, their confidence grows, making them more likely to tackle future challenges with optimism rather than fear. This pattern continues into adulthood, where they're better equipped to handle workplace dynamics, build meaningful relationships, and make important life decisions.

When my child Tori was eight, she came to me with an ambitious plan to reorganize her entire bedroom by herself. My initial impulse was to jump in and help, knowing it would be a massive undertaking for someone her age. Instead, I remembered the principles of supported independence and simply said, 'That sounds like a big project. I'm here if you need me.' Over the next three days, I watched as she methodically sorted through her belongings, occasionally asking for help with heavy items or seeking advice about storage solutions. There were moments of frustration and chaos. At one point, her room looked like a tornado had hit it, but I resisted the urge to take over. When she finally finished, her pride was palpable. More importantly, something shifted in our relationship. She began coming to me more often to share her thoughts and plans, knowing I would listen without immediately taking control. That bedroom project became a turning point in our relationship, demonstrating how stepping back actually brought us closer together.

The beauty of this approach lies in its lasting impact on parent-child relationships. When children feel trusted to handle age-appropriate challenges, they're more likely to seek parental guidance for bigger life decisions. They view their parents as trusted advisors rather than authority figures to rebel against, creating stronger, more enduring family bonds that last well into adulthood.

As we explore this chapter, we'll discover practical strategies for fostering independence while maintaining strong emotional connections. We'll learn how to recognize opportunities for stepping back, how to manage our own anxiety about letting go, and how to create an environment where independence and emotional bonds can flourish together. Most importantly, we'll see how this approach helps prepare our children not just for immediate challenges, but for a lifetime of confident decision-making and healthy relationships.

The Trust-Independence Cycle: How Autonomy Builds Stronger Bonds

At its core, the relationship between trust and independence forms an elegant cycle that shapes not just childhood development but a lifetime of emotional growth. When we trust our children with age-appropriate independence, they develop confidence in their abilities, which in turn strengthens our emotional bonds rather than weakening them. This dynamic creates a powerful foundation for both immediate growth and long-term success.

Consider Marco, a reserved 10-year-old whose parents initially handled all his social arrangements. When they began letting him manage his own playdates, first by calling friends himself, then by organizing small gatherings, they noticed something remarkable. Not only did Marco's social confidence grow, but he also became more open with them about his friendships, seeking their advice rather than their intervention. His growing independence actually deepened their family connection.

This cycle begins in early childhood but extends well into adolescence and beyond. Take the case of Jane, who at age 14 wanted to start a small jewelry-making business online. Her parents, rather than taking over or dismissing the idea, helped her research safety guidelines and market regulations, then stepped back to let her manage the venture. While she faced several early setbacks, including some negative reviews and inventory management challenges, the experience taught her valuable lessons about resilience and problem-solving. More importantly, she knew she could count on her parents for guidance without fear of them taking control.

The trust-independence cycle works most effectively when parents maintain what I call 'supportive distance,' being emotionally available while allowing children to navigate challenges appropriate to their age and abilities. This might mean letting a six-year-old resolve a playground dispute while staying within eyesight, or helping a teenager think through college applications without dictating their choices. Each successful experience builds confidence and strengthens family bonds.

What makes this cycle particularly powerful is its impact on critical thinking and decision-making skills. When children know their parents trust them to handle age-appropriate challenges, they develop better judgment and problem-solving abilities. They learn to assess situations, consider consequences, and make thoughtful choices; skills that become increasingly valuable as they move into adulthood and career planning.

The key lies in understanding that trust and independence aren't opposing forces but complementary ones. Every time we step back and allow our children to tackle manageable challenges, we communicate our confidence in their abilities. This confidence becomes a self-fulfilling prophecy, encouraging them to approach future challenges with optimism rather than fear. The trust we show in their capabilities today shapes how they'll approach decisions and relationships throughout their lives.

Parents can strengthen this cycle through several practical approaches. Start by identifying age-appropriate opportunities for independence, whether it's letting a young child choose their outfit or allowing a teenager to manage their homework schedule. Celebrate efforts and learning experiences rather than just successes. Maintain emotional availability while resisting the urge to jump in and solve problems. Most importantly, view mistakes not as failures but as valuable learning opportunities that build resilience and judgment.

This approach produces remarkable results in preparing children for adult life. Young adults who grew up with supported independence often show greater initiative in their careers, stronger relationship skills, and better emotional regulation. They're more likely to take calculated risks, innovate in their chosen fields, and maintain healthy boundaries in personal and professional relationships.

Remember that building this cycle takes time and consistency. There will be moments of doubt and anxiety for both parents and children. But by maintaining faith in the process and focusing on the long-term benefits of supported independence, we create the conditions for both immediate growth and lasting emotional resilience. This investment in our children's autonomy, while sometimes challenging, yields returns that last a lifetime.

Creating Secure Attachment Through Supported Independence

The path to secure attachment reveals a beautiful paradox: the more we trust our children with age-appropriate independence, the stronger our emotional bonds become. This principle becomes evident in countless everyday moments, from a toddler's first steps away from their parent's arms to a teenager's first solo drive. Each step toward independence, when supported with emotional availability and trust, reinforces rather than diminishes the parent-child connection.

Consider Elena, whose journey with her five-year-old son Tristan transformed their relationship. Initially, Tristan struggled with separation anxiety at school drop-offs, and Elena's instinct was to linger longer each morning. Through our work together, she learned to establish a confident, loving goodbye routine while resisting the urge to prolong her departure. Within weeks, Tristan began showing not just greater independence at school, but also more emotional openness at home, freely sharing his daily experiences and feelings with his mother.

This dynamic illustrates a crucial truth: secure attachment flourishes when children feel both the freedom to explore and the certainty of their parents' emotional availability. Like a young bird learning to fly, children need both the encouragement to leave the nest and the assurance that they can return for support when needed. This balance creates what I call the 'confidence-connection loop.' Each successful independent experience strengthens their trust in both themselves and their relationship with their parents.

The approach becomes particularly powerful as children enter their teenage years. Take sixteen-year-old Charlie, who approached his parents about wanting to take a summer job. Rather than immediately jumping into arrange employment or dismissing the idea as premature, his parents helped him research opportunities and discuss potential challenges, then stepped back to let him handle the application and interview process. When he encountered setbacks, they offered emotional support without taking over. This experience not only built Charlie's professional confidence but also deepened his trust in his parents as reliable advisors rather than controlling figures.

Creating secure attachment through supported independence requires parents to develop what I call 'strategic presence,' being emotionally available while consciously creating space for independent growth. This might mean sitting quietly nearby while a child works through a difficult homework problem, or remaining calmly accessible by phone while a teenager navigates their first solo outing with friends. The key lies in communicating both confidence in their abilities and unwavering emotional support.

This approach yields particularly strong results in developing critical life skills. Children who experience supported independence tend to develop better decision-making abilities, stronger emotional regulation, and more effective communication skills. They learn to trust their judgment while maintaining healthy relationships with family and peers; essential capabilities for success in both personal and professional spheres.

The process extends naturally into career planning and life decisions. Young adults who grew up with this balance of independence and secure attachment often show greater initiative in pursuing their goals while maintaining strong family connections. They're more likely to seek parental guidance on major life decisions, not out of dependency, but from a place of trust and respect.

Building secure attachment through supported independence isn't about perfect execution; it's about consistent presence coupled with gradual release of control. Each family's journey will look different, shaped by their unique circumstances and challenges. What remains constant is the need to balance protection with freedom, guidance with autonomy, and love with trust.

As children grow, this foundation of secure attachment through supported independence becomes increasingly valuable. It creates resilient individuals who can navigate life's challenges with confidence while maintaining meaningful connections with family. This approach doesn't just prepare children for independence; it equips them with the emotional tools to build lasting, healthy relationships throughout their lives.

Balancing Emotional Availability with Space for Growth

Finding the sweet spot between emotional presence and independence is like learning to dance; it requires rhythm, awareness, and the confidence to sometimes take a step back. Through countless family sessions, I've discovered that children thrive not when we're constantly hovering, but when they know we're reliably present while having the space to develop their own emotional capabilities.

Last year, I worked with Lisa and her 13-year-old daughter Jasmine, who was struggling with academic stress. Lisa's pattern had been to immediately jump in with solutions whenever Jasmine expressed anxiety about schoolwork. While well-intentioned, this approach was actually preventing Jasmine from developing her own coping strategies. Together, we worked on a different approach - what I call 'conscious presence.' Lisa learned to remain emotionally available without automatically providing solutions. When Jasmine would share her concerns, Lisa would acknowledge her feelings while gently encouraging her to explore potential solutions herself.

The transformation was remarkable. Within months, Jasmine began developing her own stress management techniques, like breaking large assignments into smaller tasks and using breathing exercises she'd discovered online. More importantly, she started coming to her mother not just with problems, but with ideas about how to solve them, knowing she had a supportive sounding board rather than a ready-made solution.

This balance between availability and space becomes particularly crucial as children move toward career decisions and adult life. Consider Dean, a high school junior initially paralyzed by the college selection process. His parents resisted the urge to take control, instead creating what I call a 'guided exploration space.' They remained engaged and supportive while letting Dean lead the research process, discover his own preferences, and even make some initial mistakes in his application strategy. This approach not only led to better-informed college choices but also equipped Dean with valuable decision-making skills he'll use throughout his career.

The key lies in understanding that emotional availability isn't about constant intervention; it's about creating a secure base from which children can explore and grow. Think of it like a home base in a game of tag; children venture out more confidently when they know there's a safe place to return to, but the game only works if they're free to run and play.

This balance impacts how children approach future challenges and relationships. Those who experience this combination of emotional security and independence typically develop stronger problem-solving skills, better emotional regulation, and more confidence in their ability to handle life's obstacles. They're more likely to take healthy risks in their careers and maintain balanced relationships in adulthood.

Parents can nurture this balance through several practical approaches. First, establish regular check-in times rather than constant monitoring, allowing children to develop their own rhythms of seeking support. Practice active listening without immediately offering solutions, using phrases like 'What do you think might work?' or 'Would you like to brainstorm some ideas together?' Create safe spaces for emotional expression while respecting growing independence, especially during teenage years.

Remember that this balance looks different at various developmental stages. For younger children, it might mean staying within eyesight while they navigate playground conflicts. For teenagers, it could involve being available for conversation while respecting their privacy and increasing need for autonomy. The goal remains constant: maintaining emotional connection while fostering independence.

This approach particularly benefits children as they move into career planning and adult decision-making. Young adults who experienced this balance often show greater initiative in their professional lives while maintaining healthy family connections. They're more likely to seek advice when needed but trust their judgment in making important life choices.

Implementing this balance requires parents to manage their own anxiety about stepping back. It's natural to want to protect our children from all discomfort, but managing this impulse is crucial for their emotional growth. Consider keeping a 'stepping back journal' to track moments when resisting the urge to intervene led to positive growth in your child's capabilities.

The ultimate goal is to raise children who feel emotionally secure enough to take risks, make mistakes, and forge their own paths while knowing they have a reliable support system to turn to when needed. This foundation of balanced support creates resilient adults who can navigate life's challenges with confidence while maintaining meaningful connections with others. As we close this chapter on the connection paradox, it's clear that the strongest parent-child bonds aren't built through constant intervention, but through the delicate dance of presence and trust. The stories we've explored demonstrate how stepping back thoughtfully creates space for both independence and deeper emotional connections that serve children well into adulthood.

The journey of fostering independence while maintaining strong emotional bonds transforms not just our children's present capabilities but shapes their future success in relationships, careers, and life decisions. We've seen how children who learn to navigate challenges with supported independence develop stronger critical thinking abilities and emotional resilience that benefit them long-term. Whether it's Jamie finding her own solution to researching colleges and careers or Charlie considering a summer job, these experiences build the foundation for confident decision-making and healthy relationships throughout life.

The trust-independence cycle we've explored shows how giving children age-appropriate autonomy actually strengthens family bonds rather than weakening them. Each time we step back thoughtfully while remaining emotionally available, we communicate our faith in our children's abilities while assuring them of our unwavering support. This balance creates emotionally resilient individuals who are more likely to take calculated risks, innovate in their chosen fields, and maintain healthy boundaries in both personal and professional relationships.

Moving forward, consider these essential insights:

- Trust and independence aren't opposing forces but complementary ones that strengthen emotional bonds
- Creating 'strategic presence,' being emotionally available while consciously creating space for growth, builds both confidence and connection
- Each successfully navigated challenge builds decision-making abilities that serve children well into adulthood
- The courage to step back today creates more resilient, capable individuals tomorrow

As you continue implementing these principles, remember that this journey isn't about perfect execution; it's about consistent presence coupled with gradual releasing of control. Whether you're helping a young child manage playground dynamics or supporting a teenager's career exploration, maintaining emotional availability while honoring independence creates the foundation for lasting family bonds and individual success.

In our next chapter, we'll explore how to read and respond to your child's emotional signals, building on this foundation of balanced support and independence. Until then, remember that the strongest connections grow not from doing everything for our children, but from being there while they learn to do things for themselves.

Chapter 8:

Red Flags and Green Lights: Reading Your Child's Emotional Signals

"There are only two lasting bequests we can hope to give our children. One of these is roots, the other, wings."
— *Hodding Carter Jr.*

Every child's emotional landscape tells a unique story through behaviors, reactions, and patterns that emerge over time. As parents, our ability to read and respond to these emotional signals can make the difference between fostering resilience and missing crucial opportunities for support and growth. These signals act as a sophisticated language that, when properly interpreted, guides us in nurturing our children's emotional development while fostering their independence. Like learning any new language, becoming fluent in reading emotional signals takes time and practice, but the rewards are immeasurable for both parent and child.

Through my years of working with families, I've witnessed how understanding emotional signals transforms not just parenting approaches, but entire family dynamics. Consider the story of Paul, a quiet 10-year-old whose parents initially interpreted his withdrawal from soccer as simple disinterest. However, by paying closer attention to his emotional signals, particularly his enthusiasm when playing one-on-one with friends versus his tension before team practices, they discovered he was struggling with performance anxiety rather than disliking the sport. Instead of either forcing continued participation or allowing him to quit, they helped him develop coping strategies while gradually rebuilding his confidence through smaller group activities.

Recognizing emotional signals isn't just about identifying potential challenges; it's equally about spotting opportunities for growth and independence. When parents learn to identify their child's 'ready signals,' they can better support natural progression toward emotional maturity. These signals might appear as subtle as a previously hesitant child showing curiosity about a new situation, or as direct as a teenager assertively expressing their viewpoint during family discussions.

Crucial to this understanding is recognizing how emotional signals evolve as children grow. A toddler's tantrum speaks a different emotional language than a teenager's quiet withdrawal, yet both carry important messages about their internal experiences and developing needs. These signals often provide windows into our children's readiness for new challenges or their need for additional support in developing critical life skills like decision-making and problem-solving.

In this chapter, we'll explore how to develop what I call your 'emotional signal radar,' the ability to distinguish between moments that require your intervention and opportunities for your child to develop resilience through managing challenges independently. We'll examine how various emotional signals manifest across different age groups and situations, from academic challenges to social interactions, and how these signals often indicate your child's readiness for greater independence or their need for additional support.

Most importantly, we'll focus on practical strategies for responding to these signals in ways that support both emotional growth and the development of critical thinking skills. You'll learn how to create an environment where your child feels safe expressing their emotions while gradually building the confidence to handle increasingly complex situations on their own. This balanced approach helps prepare them not just for immediate challenges, but for future success in relationships, career choices, and life decisions.

Through understanding your child's emotional signals, you're not just supporting their current development; you're helping them build the emotional intelligence and resilience they'll need throughout their lives. This skill becomes particularly valuable as they approach major life transitions, from starting school to choosing a career path, where their ability to recognize and trust their own emotional signals will guide them toward authentic and fulfilling choices.

Understanding the Difference: Normal Development vs. Warning Signs

Understanding emotional development means recognizing that each child's path is uniquely their own. While one child might boldly face new social situations at age five, another may need more time to warm up; both approaches can reflect healthy development. What matters most is not how quickly children reach emotional milestones, but that they're steadily developing the tools they need for emotional resilience and independence.

Take Samantha's story with her 6-year-old son, Alfie. She noticed he became extremely upset when losing at board games, while his older sister had always handled competition well at that age. During our sessions, we explored how Alfie's reactions, though intense, were actually helping him learn valuable emotional skills as he worked through disappointment. Rather than avoiding games or letting him win, Samantha learned to support him through these moments, helping him identify his feelings and develop coping strategies. By age seven, Alfie had not only improved his emotional regulation but had developed valuable problem-solving skills that extended into other areas of his life.

When assessing your child's emotional development, consider the whole picture rather than isolated incidents. A child who occasionally expresses worry about a test is showing normal development; one who consistently experiences physical symptoms of anxiety about school may need additional support. Look for patterns and progress over time, emotional growth isn't linear, and temporary regressions during stress or life changes are normal.

Green light signals of healthy emotional development include a child's ability to recover from setbacks with appropriate support, maintain friendships despite occasional conflicts, and show interest in solving problems independently. Watch for their growing capacity to express emotions verbally, even if imperfectly, and their willingness to try new experiences after initial hesitation. These indicators suggest your child is building crucial emotional skills that will serve them throughout life.

However, certain behaviors warrant closer attention. Persistent withdrawal from previously enjoyed activities, dramatic changes in sleep or eating patterns, or frequent physical complaints without a medical cause may signal emotional challenges requiring professional support. The key is understanding context, a child who's temporarily less social following a move is different from one who consistently struggles to connect with peers.

Critical thinking and decision-making abilities develop alongside emotional growth. When children face age-appropriate challenges, they build mental frameworks for handling future situations. For instance, allowing a middle-schooler to manage their homework schedule, even if they occasionally miss assignments, helps them develop time management skills they'll need in high school and beyond. These experiences contribute to their ability to make sound decisions about their future, including career choices and personal relationships.

Consider the experience of twelve-year-old Laura, who initially struggled with the transition to middle school. Instead of immediately intervening when she forgot assignments, her parents helped her develop her own organizational system. Though she experienced some academic setbacks initially, she emerged with stronger problem-solving skills and greater confidence in her ability to handle challenges independently. This foundation of self-reliance will serve her well as she faces bigger decisions about her education and career path.

Remember that emotional development encompasses more than just managing feelings - it's about building a toolkit for life success. A child who learns to regulate emotions, think critically about challenges, and make independent decisions is developing the resilience and judgment needed for future endeavors. Whether choosing a college major or navigating workplace relationships, these early emotional lessons lay the groundwork for confident decision-making throughout life.

When supporting your child's emotional development, focus on creating opportunities for guided independence rather than protecting them from all discomfort. This approach helps them develop the confidence to handle increasingly complex situations while knowing they have support when truly needed. The goal isn't to eliminate struggle but to help children develop the tools to navigate life's challenges successfully.

Green Light Moments: Recognizing and Celebrating Emotional Growth

Identifying and celebrating moments of emotional growth isn't just about marking milestones; it's about recognizing your child's developing capacity for independence, resilience, and self-awareness. These green light moments often appear in everyday situations, signaling that your child is ready for greater emotional responsibility and independence.

Consider 9-year-old Ryan's experience at summer camp. Initially anxious about being away from home, he developed his own bedtime routine to manage homesickness, looking at family photos, writing in his journal, and using breathing exercises we'd practiced. When his parents visited on parents' day, instead of immediately running to them, he proudly showed them around 'his' camp, introducing his new friends and explaining his coping strategies. This wasn't just about adapting to camp; it demonstrated Ryan's growing emotional intelligence and independence.

Green light moments manifest differently across age groups and personalities. For a toddler, it might be finding words to express frustration instead of having a tantrum. For a teenager, it could mean thoughtfully weighing the pros and cons of joining a new activity rather than making impulsive decisions. These moments show our children are developing critical thinking skills and emotional wisdom they'll carry into adulthood.

The key to recognizing these moments lies in understanding that they often emerge from challenges. When 12-year-old Paula experienced conflict with her best friend, instead of immediately intervening, her mother watched as Paula navigated the situation herself. Paula reflected on the disagreement, considered her friend's perspective, and initiated a conversation to resolve their differences. This demonstrated not just emotional maturity but the kind of problem-solving skills essential for future relationships and career success.

Celebrating these moments requires a delicate touch. Instead of lavish praise that might create dependency on external validation, focus on acknowledging the process and growth you observe. A simple 'I noticed how you thought about different solutions before deciding what to do' can be more meaningful than 'Good job!' This approach helps children internalize the value of emotional growth and build confidence in their decision-making abilities.

Pay attention to subtle signs of emotional development. When your previously cautious child volunteers to present in class, or your impulsive teenager pauses to consider consequences before acting, these are green light moments worth noting. These shifts often indicate growing emotional intelligence and readiness for new challenges.

Document these moments in ways that resonate with your child's age and personality. For younger children, a 'growth journal' with pictures and stories can make emotional progress tangible. For teenagers, periodic reflection conversations about how they've handled recent challenges differently than they might have in the past can reinforce their developing emotional capabilities.

Remember that emotional growth isn't linear. Children may show remarkable emotional wisdom in one situation while struggling in another. The goal isn't perfection but progress. When 7-year-old Alfie successfully managed his disappointment at losing a game but later melted down over a change in plans, his parents recognized that emotional development happens in waves, not straight lines.

These green light moments extend beyond childhood, laying the foundation for crucial life skills. A teenager who learns to advocate for themselves respectfully with teachers is developing communication skills they'll use in college and their career. A child who learns to identify and express their emotions clearly is building relationship skills that will serve them throughout life.

As you recognize these moments, consider how they contribute to your child's broader journey toward independence. Each healthy emotional response, thoughtful decision, or show of empathy represents a step toward becoming a resilient, emotionally intelligent adult capable of navigating relationships, career challenges, and life's inevitable ups and downs with confidence and wisdom.

When to Seek Support: Guidelines for Professional Intervention

Supporting your child's emotional development often means finding the delicate balance between allowing natural growth and recognizing when professional guidance becomes necessary. Through my years of working with families, I've learned that seeking professional support isn't a sign of parental failure; it's often a demonstration of wisdom and commitment to your child's well-being.

Consider the story of eleven-year-old Phil, whose parents noticed gradual changes in his behavior over several months. Once outgoing and engaged, he became increasingly withdrawn from activities he previously enjoyed. His mother initially wondered if this was typical pre-teen behavior, but her instincts told her something more was happening. After observing the persistence and impact of these changes on Phil's daily life, his parents decided to seek professional guidance. This decision led to discovering underlying anxiety issues that, once addressed, helped Phil regain his confidence and develop valuable coping skills.

Certain patterns and behaviors often signal the need for professional support. When emotional responses consistently interfere with daily functioning, affecting sleep, appetite, social interactions, or academic performance, it's appropriate to seek professional guidance. The key is looking for persistence and impact rather than isolated incidents. A child who occasionally feels nervous about tests is experiencing normal emotions; one who develops physical symptoms preventing school attendance may need additional support.

Watch for significant changes in your child's typical behavior patterns. This might include withdrawal from previously enjoyed activities, dramatic mood shifts, difficulty maintaining friendships, or persistent negative self-talk. Pay particular attention when these changes last longer than two weeks and affect multiple areas of life: home, school, and social relationships.

Immediate professional intervention becomes necessary when safety concerns arise. If your child expresses thoughts of self-harm, shows aggressive behavior that poses risks, or experiences trauma, don't wait to seek help. These situations require prompt attention from qualified professionals who can provide appropriate support and guidance.

Your parental intuition plays a vital role in identifying when professional help might be beneficial. Parents who maintain strong emotional connections with their children often notice subtle changes that signal emotional distress. Trust your instincts while remaining mindful of your child's overall development, both as an individual and in relation to their peers.

When considering professional support, start by gathering specific observations about patterns or concerns. Rather than general statements like 'something seems wrong,' note specific behaviors, their frequency, and impact on daily life. This information helps professionals better understand your child's needs and develop effective support strategies.

Remember that seeking professional guidance is about adding tools to your parenting toolkit, not replacing your role in your child's emotional development. Professional support can help identify underlying issues, provide targeted strategies, and offer perspectives that complement your parenting approach. This collaborative approach often leads to more effective outcomes.

Professional support comes in various forms, from school counselors and child psychologists to family therapists and pediatric mental health specialists. Each offers different expertise and approaches, allowing you to find the best match for your child's specific needs. The goal is to find someone who can work effectively with both you and your child while respecting your family's values and parenting style.

Most importantly, seeking professional support early often prevents smaller challenges from becoming larger issues. It demonstrates to your child that asking for help is a sign of strength, not weakness. This lesson in emotional intelligence and self-awareness serves them well throughout life, particularly as they face future decisions about education, careers, and relationships.

As your child grows, professional support might be beneficial during major life transitions or when facing significant challenges. Whether it's adjusting to a new school, dealing with family changes, or navigating social pressures, having professional guidance can help develop valuable coping strategies while building resilience for future challenges. As we conclude this vital exploration of reading emotional signals, remember that understanding your child's emotional language is both an art and a skill that grows stronger with mindful practice. Throughout this chapter, we've seen how interpreting these signals goes far beyond identifying potential problems; it's about recognizing opportunities for growth, building decision-making abilities, and fostering the confidence that comes from healthy independence.

The journey of reading emotional signals teaches us that our children's capacity for emotional growth often exceeds our expectations. Like Paul learning to manage performance anxiety through gradual exposure, or Alfie developing ways to manage playing board games without meltdowns, each challenge presents an opportunity for developing critical thinking skills and emotional resilience that will serve them well into adulthood. These experiences lay the foundation for future success, whether they're choosing a career path, navigating professional relationships, or making important life decisions.

Your role in this process is not to eliminate all emotional challenges but to create a supportive environment where your child feels safe experiencing and processing emotions while developing their own solutions. By maintaining this balance, you help build not just emotional intelligence but also the critical thinking and decision-making abilities essential for lifelong success.

Moving forward, challenge yourself to step back and observe more than you intervene. Notice the subtle signs of emotional growth, celebrate the moments of independent problem-solving, and trust that your child is developing the emotional tools they need. When intervention is necessary, approach it with the goal of guiding rather than controlling, always keeping in mind that each emotional challenge successfully navigated builds confidence and resilience.

In our next chapter, we'll explore how these emotional signals and responses evolve across different developmental stages, providing stage-specific strategies for supporting emotional growth from toddlerhood through adolescence. Until then, remember that becoming fluent in your child's emotional language is a journey that strengthens not just their emotional intelligence but the bond you share as they grow into confident, capable individuals.

Chapter 9:

From Toddler to Teen: Stage-Specific Strategies for Emotional Growth

"The greatest gifts you can give your children are the roots of responsibility and the wings of independence."
— *Denis Waitley*

The journey from toddlerhood to adolescence represents one of the most dramatic transformations in human emotional development, with each stage bringing its own unique challenges and opportunities for growth. As parents, our role must evolve just as dramatically, from being the primary emotional regulators for our toddlers to becoming trusted emotional consultants for our teens. Each developmental stage brings its own set of unique emotional landscapes to navigate, from a toddler learning to express basic needs to a teenager grappling with complex social dynamics and identity formation. These transitions aren't just challenging for our children; they require us as parents to continually evolve our approach, adapting our support strategies while gradually expanding the boundaries of independence.

Consider how a child's decision-making abilities develop: at age four, they might choose their daily outfit; by twelve, they're managing their homework schedule; and as teens, they're weighing important social and academic choices that will shape their future. This progression in emotional maturity and decision-making capability doesn't just happen naturally; it requires intentional parenting that creates space for both growth and guided support.

What makes this journey particularly challenging is that emotional development rarely follows a linear path. A teenager who confidently manages complex school projects might still struggle with basic emotional regulation during family conflicts. A ten-year-old showing remarkable empathy with friends might revert to toddler-like behavior when overtired. These apparent contradictions aren't signs of regression but rather natural oscillations in the emotional growth process.

The key lies in recognizing these developmental stages not as rigid categories but as fluid transitions, each building upon the foundations laid in earlier years. The emotional tools we help our children develop in elementary school, like basic problem-solving and self-regulation, become the building blocks for handling more complex emotional challenges in adolescence. These skills ultimately shape how they'll approach relationships, career decisions, and life challenges in adulthood.

Through my years of working with families, I've observed how this stage-specific approach to emotional development creates more resilient, confident individuals. Children who are allowed to experience age-appropriate challenges while having access to parental support tend to develop stronger decision-making abilities, greater emotional intelligence, and more effective problem-solving skills. These capabilities serve them well beyond childhood, influencing their future relationships, career choices, and ability to navigate life's inevitable challenges.

In this chapter, we'll explore specific strategies for supporting emotional growth at each developmental stage, helping you recognize when to step in and when to step back. We'll examine how to adjust your parenting approach as your child matures, ensuring you're providing the right balance of support and independence at every age. You'll learn practical tools for fostering emotional intelligence, building resilience, and nurturing critical thinking skills that will serve your child throughout their life journey.

Understanding Stage-Specific Emotional Needs: From Tantrums to Teen Angst

Just as a house needs different types of support at various stages of construction, children require distinct forms of emotional scaffolding as they develop. Understanding these stage-specific needs helps us provide appropriate support while fostering independence and resilience.

During the toddler years (ages 1-3), children experience emotions with an intensity that can feel overwhelming, both for them and their caregivers. A simple 'no' might trigger what seems like an emotional tsunami. Instead of immediately trying to stop these emotional expressions, our role is to provide a calm presence and help name these big feelings. When three-year-old Matilda had a meltdown because her sandwich was cut into squares instead of triangles, her father resisted the urge to immediately 'fix' the situation. Instead, he acknowledged her feelings: 'You're feeling frustrated because your sandwich isn't the shape you wanted. That's hard.' This validation, combined with allowing her to experience and move through the emotion, helped Matilda develop early emotional regulation skills.

Early childhood (ages 4-7) brings expanding emotional vocabulary and social awareness. Children at this stage are beginning to recognize that others have different perspectives and feelings from their own. This is the perfect time to help them develop emotional intelligence and basic problem-solving skills. When six-year-old Adam came home upset because his best friend wouldn't share toys during playtime, his mother used it as an opportunity to explore different perspectives and brainstorm solutions. Rather than immediately scheduling a playdate with another friend or calling the other parent, she helped Adam think through how his friend might have been feeling and what solutions he could try next time.

Middle childhood (ages 8-12) marks a significant shift toward emotional independence as peer relationships become increasingly complex. Children at this stage need guidance in developing healthy boundaries and conflict resolution skills while being given space to navigate social dynamics. When ten-year-old Jackie struggled with a friendship group that kept changing the rules about who could join their lunch table, her parents resisted solving the problem for her. Instead, they helped her explore her values and develop strategies for either addressing the situation or finding new friendship opportunities.

The teenage years (13-18) bring perhaps the most nuanced emotional landscape. Teens are developing abstract thinking abilities that allow them to grapple with complex emotional and moral questions while their brains are still developing impulse control and decision-making capabilities. They need parents to transition from problem-solvers to trusted consultants; available for support but not jumping in to rescue them from every challenge. When sixteen-year-old Ian was stressed about juggling sports commitments with academic pressure, his parents helped him analyze his priorities and supported him in making his own decisions about time management.

Throughout these stages, children need opportunities to develop critical thinking and decision-making skills that will serve them in adulthood. A toddler deciding which snack to eat, a grade-schooler managing their homework routine, or a teenager weighing the pros and cons of different summer job opportunities; each experience builds confidence and competence.

Remember that emotional development isn't strictly linear. A child who shows remarkable emotional maturity in one situation might struggle with basic emotional regulation in another context. The key is maintaining consistent support while adjusting our approach to match their current developmental needs and capabilities.

This stage-specific understanding helps us create an environment where children can develop emotional resilience, self-awareness, and problem-solving skills naturally. Whether it's a four-year-old learning to wait their turn or a teenager navigating complex social dynamics, each stage offers unique opportunities for growth when we provide the right balance of support and independence.

Adapting Your Parenting Style: When to Hold On and When to Let Go

Adapting your parenting style is much like teaching a child to swim. At first, you keep a gentle hand under their back, guiding them through the water and ensuring they feel safe. Over time, as their confidence and skills grow, you gradually let your support drift away; watching closely, ready to step in if needed, but allowing them the space to paddle on their own. This ongoing shift between support and independence requires constant awareness and adjustment, matching your guidance to their growing abilities and needs.

Consider the story of Martin, a bright 12-year-old who struggled with organizing his schoolwork. His mother, Rebecca, had always managed his assignments, checked his backpack, and reminded him of due dates. When Martin entered middle school, this system began to break down as the workload increased. During our sessions, Rebecca realized her helpful intentions were actually preventing Martin from developing crucial executive functioning skills. We created a gradual transition plan where Rebeca stepped back while remaining emotionally available. The first month was challenging, Martin forgot several assignments and received some lower grades. However, this experience motivated him to develop his own organizational system. By semester's end, he was tracking assignments independently and showing pride in managing his responsibilities. More importantly, this newfound independence strengthened his relationship with Rebecca, as she shifted from manager to mentor.

The key to adapting your parenting style lies in recognizing your child's growing capabilities while remaining emotionally present. This means allowing them to experience appropriate challenges while providing a safety net for significant struggles. For younger children, this might mean letting them choose their own clothes (even if they don't match) or allowing them to pack their own lunch (with guidance about nutritional choices). For teenagers, it could involve letting them manage their own schedule, including experiencing the natural consequences of poor time management.

The process requires parents to develop new skills as well. Instead of jumping in with solutions, practice asking questions that encourage problem-solving: 'What do you think you could try next?' or 'How might you handle this differently next time?' This approach helps children develop critical thinking skills while maintaining your supportive presence.

Consider emotional regulation as another area where parenting style must evolve. When your toddler has a meltdown, direct intervention and co-regulation are appropriate. However, as your child grows, your role shifts toward helping them recognize their emotional states and develop their own coping strategies. This progression builds emotional intelligence and self-reliance that serves them well into adulthood.

The transition isn't just about stepping back; it's about stepping into a different role. As children mature, parents become more like consultants, offering guidance when asked while respecting their growing autonomy. This shift particularly impacts how children approach decision-making about their future. When teenagers feel supported in making age-appropriate choices, they develop confidence in their ability to navigate life's challenges and make sound decisions about their education, career, and relationships.

Remember that adapting your style doesn't mean abandoning your child to figure everything out alone. Rather, it means being intentional about how and when you offer support. Think of it as moving from being the captain of their ship to becoming their harbor, a safe place they can return to for guidance and support while learning to navigate their own course.

This evolution in parenting style also helps children develop resilience through experiencing and managing appropriate challenges. When parents adjust their support to match their child's developmental stage, they create opportunities for growth through natural consequences while maintaining emotional security. This balance helps children build the confidence and competence they need for future success.

The ultimate goal is to help our children develop into emotionally intelligent, self-reliant adults who can navigate life's challenges with confidence. By thoughtfully adapting our parenting style, knowing when to hold on and when to let go, we create space for this natural progression while maintaining the strong emotional bonds that support healthy development.

Building Emotional Scaffolding: Age-Appropriate Tools for Self-Regulation

Just as children need physical support while learning to walk, they require emotional scaffolding as they develop self-regulation skills. This scaffolding evolves with age, providing the right level of support while gradually transferring responsibility for emotional management to the child themselves.

For toddlers and preschoolers (ages 2-5), emotional scaffolding starts with simple tools that help them identify and express feelings. Consider four-year-old Daisy, who struggled with transitions between activities. Instead of rushing to fix her distress, her parents introduced a 'feelings thermometer,' a visual tool that helped her communicate the intensity of her emotions. They also created a special 'calm down corner' with sensory items like squeeze balls and breathing buddies. These concrete tools gave Daisy a way to begin managing her emotions independently while knowing support was available when needed.

Elementary-age children (6-10) are ready for more sophisticated emotional regulation strategies. When eight-year-old Will faced frustration with challenging math problems, his parents helped him develop a three-step approach: identify the feeling ('I'm getting frustrated'), use a calming strategy (count to ten or take three deep breaths), and choose a solution (ask for help or take a short break). This framework gave Will a reliable process for managing similar situations independently, building his confidence in handling emotional challenges.

For tweens (11-13), emotional scaffolding focuses on developing more nuanced understanding and response patterns. They're ready to learn about how thoughts influence feelings and behaviors. Take twelve-year-old Catherine, who felt overwhelmed by social media comparisons. Rather than banning social media, her parents helped her develop critical thinking skills to examine these feelings and create healthy boundaries. They introduced journaling as a tool for processing complex emotions and taught her to recognize when she needed to step back from triggering situations.

Teenagers (14-18) need scaffolding that acknowledges their growing independence while providing support for increasingly complex emotional challenges. Instead of prescribing solutions, parents can help teens develop their own emotional regulation toolkit. This might include stress management techniques for academic pressure, strategies for navigating relationship dynamics, or methods for balancing various responsibilities. The goal is to help them build a personalized set of coping skills they can carry into adulthood.

Decision-making skills develop alongside emotional regulation abilities. For younger children, this might mean choosing between two calming activities when upset. As they mature, they learn to make more complex choices about managing their emotional responses and seeking appropriate support when needed. This progression helps build the critical thinking and problem-solving abilities essential for future success in relationships, careers, and life challenges.

The key to effective emotional scaffolding lies in its flexibility. Just as physical scaffolding is adjusted as a building grows, emotional support must adapt to meet changing developmental needs. Sometimes this means stepping back to allow for independent problem-solving, while other times it requires being more present during particularly challenging situations. The goal isn't to eliminate emotional challenges but to provide appropriate support for children to develop their own regulation skills.

Remember that progress isn't always linear. A teenager who usually manages emotions well might occasionally need more basic support during times of stress. This regression is normal and provides opportunities to reinforce foundational emotional regulation skills while respecting their growing maturity. Each experience builds resilience and contributes to their emotional intelligence toolkit.

Emotional scaffolding also includes teaching children to recognize when they need support. This self-awareness becomes particularly important as they move toward independence and begin making decisions about their future. Understanding when and how to seek help, whether from parents, mentors, or professional resources, is a crucial life skill that serves them well beyond childhood.

Through consistent and age-appropriate emotional scaffolding, children develop the self-regulation skills needed to navigate life's challenges confidently. This foundation of emotional competence influences everything from their academic success and career choices to their ability to maintain healthy relationships and cope with future challenges. As we conclude our exploration of emotional development across different life stages, it's clear that supporting our children's journey from dependence to independence requires an evolving approach that grows with them. The path from toddlerhood to adolescence isn't just about surviving each phase; it's about fostering the critical thinking, decision-making, and emotional regulation skills that will serve them throughout their lives.

The story of Will and his transition to having coping strategies to calm him down when he faced math problems, or any future issues. While the initial challenges were uncomfortable, they led to the development of crucial emotional regulation skills and a stronger parent-child relationship built on trust rather than dependence. This transformation exemplifies how appropriate emotional scaffolding can support children in developing their own problem-solving abilities while maintaining secure emotional connections.

As we've seen throughout this chapter, emotional development intertwines deeply with decision-making capabilities and critical thinking skills. When we adjust our support to match our children's developmental stage, whether it's helping a toddler name their feelings during a tantrum or supporting a teenager in weighing complex social choices, we create opportunities for genuine emotional growth and resilience. This balanced approach helps children develop the confidence to navigate future challenges, from career decisions to relationship dynamics.

Remember that emotional growth isn't about perfection or following a rigid timeline. Each stage brings unique opportunities for development, from the intense emotions of early childhood to the nuanced social dynamics of adolescence. Our role as parents evolves from being primary emotional regulators to becoming trusted consultants, creating space for our children to develop their emotional muscles through age-appropriate challenges while maintaining a supportive presence.

Carry forward these essential principles: validate emotions while encouraging problem-solving, adjust your support based on developmental needs, and trust in your child's growing capabilities. More than just managing today's emotional challenges, you're building the foundation for a lifetime of emotional resilience and effective decision-making. Your evolving role in their emotional journey shapes not only how they handle current challenges but also how they'll approach adult responsibilities and relationships.

Look ahead with confidence, knowing that each time you step back thoughtfully, you create space for your child to step forward into their own emotional capability. Trust their journey of growth, celebrate their progress in developing critical thinking and decision-making skills, and remain their emotional anchor as they navigate each new stage of development. This investment in their emotional growth today paves the way for their success in relationships, careers, and life's challenges tomorrow.

The journey of emotional development continues beyond childhood, but the tools, resilience, and self-awareness you help cultivate now will serve as the foundation for a lifetime of emotional intelligence and independent decision-making. Your thoughtful support today helps ensure your child develops into a confident, capable adult ready to navigate their own path forward.

Chapter 10:

The Confident Parent's Roadmap: Your Action Plan for Raising Resilient Kids

"The greatest glory in living lies not in never failing, but in rising every time we fail."
— Nelson Mandela

Building resilience in our children isn't about following a perfect formula; it's about creating a consistent environment where emotional growth can flourish naturally. As parents, our greatest challenge often lies not in knowing what to do, but in trusting ourselves and our children enough to step back and let natural learning take place. Throughout our journey in this book, we've explored the delicate balance between protection and independence, understanding emotional milestones, and creating environments where resilience can flourish. Now, we'll synthesize these insights into actionable strategies that work for your unique family situation. This roadmap isn't about perfection; it's about progress and creating sustainable habits that foster both emotional growth and practical life skills.

Think about building emotional resilience, like teaching your child to navigate an increasingly complex world. Just as a GPS offers multiple routes to reach a destination, your parenting journey will have various paths, each offering unique opportunities for growth. Some days, you'll take the scenic route, allowing natural consequences to be the teacher. Other times, you'll need to provide more direct guidance through challenging emotional terrain. The key is recognizing which approach serves your child's development best in each situation.

During my years working with families, I've observed that parents who successfully foster resilience share a common trait: they've learned to trust the process of gradual independence. They understand that each small step, whether it's letting their child resolve a playground dispute or manage their homework schedule, builds the foundation for future emotional strength and decision-making ability. These parents have discovered that stepping back isn't about disengaging; it's about shifting from being the primary problem-solver to becoming a trusted advisor and emotional coach.

As we explore the practical strategies in this chapter, remember that this journey isn't just about your child's growth; it's also about your evolution as a parent. You'll learn to recognize opportunities for building resilience in everyday moments, understand how to gradually expand your child's independence zones, and develop the confidence to trust both yourself and your child's natural development process. Whether you're dealing with a toddler's first attempts at self-regulation or a teenager's complex social dynamics, you'll find concrete tools to support their journey while maintaining appropriate boundaries.

Most importantly, this chapter will show you how these approaches prepare your child not just for immediate challenges, but for long-term success in their personal and professional lives. You'll see how the skills they develop now, from problem-solving and decision-making to emotional regulation and critical thinking, become the foundation for their future relationships, career choices, and life satisfaction. By fostering independence and resilience today, you're equipping them with the tools they'll need to navigate their own unique path tomorrow.

Creating Age-Appropriate Independence Zones: Setting Healthy Boundaries

Creating spaces for independence is like designing a series of expanding circles, each representing new opportunities for growth and learning. At the center lies your child's current comfort zone, those tasks and responsibilities they've already mastered. The outer edges represent their growth zone, where new challenges await, but risks remain manageable. As your child demonstrates readiness, these circles naturally expand, allowing them to tackle increasingly complex challenges while building confidence and capability.

For young children ages 3-5, independence zones often center around basic self-care and simple decision-making. A preschooler might start by choosing their clothes for the day from parent-approved options or helping to pack their snack for daycare. When four-year-old Simon began selecting his own outfits, some combinations were unconventional, like polka dots with stripes, but allowing these minor mismatches helped build his confidence in making choices. His mother noticed that this small independence led to a greater willingness to try new things in other areas.

The elementary years (ages 6-11) bring opportunities for expanding independence in academics, social relationships, and household responsibilities. Consider how nine-year-old Liza transitioned from having her parents manage her homework routine to creating her own study schedule. Initially, she struggled with time management, occasionally missing assignments. However, these natural consequences taught her more about responsibility than any parental lecture could have achieved. By year's end, she had developed her own system for tracking assignments and managing project deadlines.

Tweens and early teens (ages 12-14) require carefully calibrated independence zones that acknowledge their growing capabilities while maintaining necessary safety nets. This might include managing their own social media time within agreed-upon boundaries or taking responsibility for planning and cooking one family meal per week. When thirteen-year-old Rich expressed interest in cooking, his parents created a framework where he could experiment in the kitchen while learning about nutrition, budgeting, and meal planning. His initial attempts weren't culinary masterpieces, but the pride he felt in feeding his family was invaluable.

For older teens (15-18), independence zones should mirror the adult responsibilities they'll soon assume. This includes managing their own schedule, making decisions about extracurricular activities, and taking increased responsibility for their academic and career planning. Rather than parents micromanaging college applications, teens should drive this process while having access to parental guidance when needed. These experiences build critical thinking skills and prepare them for adult decision-making.

Remember that independence zones aren't about abandoning structure; they're about creating safe spaces for learning through experience. When sixteen-year-old Anna wanted to attend her first concert with friends, her parents helped her develop a safety plan instead of simply saying no. They discussed transportation options, meeting points, and communication expectations. This collaborative approach helped Anna feel both independent and supported.

Each expansion of independence should consider three key factors: your child's demonstrated responsibility in current zones, their emotional readiness for new challenges, and the potential natural consequences of mistakes. The goal isn't to protect them from all difficulties but to ensure that any setbacks serve as learning opportunities rather than overwhelming failures.

Monitor how your child handles current responsibilities before expanding their independence zone. Are they consistently completing current tasks? Do they show good judgment in existing decision-making opportunities? Do they recognize when to seek help? These indicators help determine readiness for new challenges. Success in managing a weekly allowance, for example, might indicate readiness for larger financial responsibilities.

Most importantly, independence zones should flex and adapt based on your child's individual development and circumstances. Some children naturally seek more independence earlier, while others need more time and support. The key is maintaining consistent boundaries while gradually expanding the scope of independence as your child demonstrates readiness for new challenges. This approach builds not just practical skills, but the confidence and resilience they'll need throughout life.

The Five-Step Resilience Building Framework

Building resilience isn't about protecting children from all challenges; it's about giving them the tools and confidence to face life's inevitable obstacles. Through years of working with families, I've developed and refined a framework that helps parents systematically build their child's emotional strength while maintaining appropriate support. This approach focuses on developing both practical skills and emotional capabilities that serve children well into adulthood.

The first step in this framework centers on creating psychological safety through predictability. When children know they have a secure emotional base, they're more willing to take healthy risks and explore their capabilities. Consider Helen, a typically cautious seven-year-old who struggled with new situations. Her parents established consistent routines and clear communication channels, helping her feel secure enough to gradually push beyond her comfort zone. This foundation of security became the springboard for her growing independence.

Step two involves identifying appropriate challenge zones: areas where children can stretch their abilities while maintaining a sense of agency. These challenges should be meaningful but manageable. For instance, when twelve-year-old Cameron expressed interest in earning money, his parents helped him start a small yard work business in their neighborhood. While they didn't manage his schedule or handle customer communications, they remained available for guidance and support. This independence within boundaries allowed Cameron to develop problem-solving skills while building confidence in his abilities.

The third step focuses on developing critical thinking through natural consequences. This means resisting the urge to rescue children from the results of their choices when those consequences aren't harmful. When fifteen-year-old Hannah repeatedly forgot her soccer gear, her parents stopped bringing it to practice. Missing one game was uncomfortable, but it led Hannah to develop her own pre-practice checklist and take ownership of her responsibilities. These experiences build decision-making muscles that serve children well in future academic and professional settings.

Step four emphasizes emotional intelligence through reflection and processing. Rather than just experiencing consequences, children need support in understanding what happened and why. After sixteen-year-old Russel missed a college application deadline, his parents helped him analyze how his time management contributed to the situation and develop strategies for future deadlines. This reflective practice builds self-awareness and improves future decision-making.

The final step involves expanding independence zones based on demonstrated readiness. As children show capability in handling current responsibilities, they earn greater autonomy in new areas. This graduated approach builds confidence while maintaining safety. For instance, when thirteen-year-old Nina consistently completed her homework independently, she earned the right to manage her own study schedule, preparing her for the increased academic independence of high school.

Implementation of this framework requires patience and consistency. Start with small opportunities for independence and gradually increase complexity as your child demonstrates readiness. Remember that setbacks aren't failures; they're learning opportunities that contribute to long-term resilience. The framework's success lies in its flexibility, adapting to different ages and personalities while maintaining core principles of supported independence.

Most importantly, this framework prepares children for future challenges beyond home and school. The problem-solving skills, emotional awareness, and confidence they develop serve them well in college, careers, and relationships. When children learn to navigate challenges with appropriate support, they develop not just resilience but also the self-trust needed to pursue their own path in life.

Consider how this approach helped fourteen-year-old Aaron navigate his first serious academic challenge. Rather than intervening when he struggled in advanced math, his parents used the framework to help him develop his own solution strategy. He learned to identify when he needed help, sought out appropriate resources, and ultimately developed study techniques that served him throughout high school and college. This experience built not just academic skills, but also the confidence to tackle future challenges independently.

The framework's emphasis on graduated independence particularly benefits children as they approach major life transitions. Whether preparing for high school, college, or career choices, they have a foundation of problem-solving experience and emotional resilience to draw upon. They know how to assess challenges, seek appropriate support, and trust their ability to navigate new situations; skills essential for success in any field they choose to pursue.

Measuring Progress: Emotional Growth Milestones and Celebrations

Think of emotional growth like watching a garden flourish; while each plant develops at its own pace, there are clear signs of progress that deserve recognition and celebration. Understanding and acknowledging these milestones not only helps parents track their child's development but also reinforces the value of emotional intelligence and personal growth.

The journey of emotional development often reveals itself in subtle yet significant ways. Consider ten-year-old Colin, who traditionally struggled with losing at games. After months of practicing emotional regulation techniques, he handled a chess tournament loss with remarkable grace, congratulating his opponent and analyzing what he could learn from the experience. This wasn't just about sportsmanship; it demonstrated growing emotional maturity and resilience that would serve him well in future challenges.

Critical thinking milestones often emerge through daily decision-making. When thirteen-year-old Jill faced a conflict between a friend's party and a long-scheduled family commitment, she independently weighed her options, considered others' feelings, and made a thoughtful choice without parental intervention. These moments of independent reasoning show growing emotional sophistication and deserve acknowledgment.

Resilience markers frequently appear during times of challenge. Fifteen-year-old Jack's response to not making the varsity team illustrated significant emotional growth. Instead of giving up, he asked the coach for feedback, created an improvement plan, and committed to additional practice, demonstrating problem-solving skills and emotional regulation that would benefit him in future career challenges.

Celebrating these developments requires a delicate touch; too much praise can create dependency on external validation, while too little might fail to reinforce positive growth. When acknowledging progress, focus on the process rather than the outcome. Instead of saying 'Good job staying calm,' try 'I noticed how you took deep breaths and thought about solutions when you felt frustrated. How did that strategy work for you?'

Independence milestones often manifest in everyday situations. When twelve-year-old Julie began proactively managing her homework schedule and seeking help when needed, it showed growing self-awareness and responsibility. These practical demonstrations of emotional maturity contribute to future success in academic and professional settings.

Document progress in ways that empower rather than evaluate. A shared journal where children can reflect on their emotional growth journey often proves more valuable than traditional tracking methods. This approach helps children develop self-awareness while giving parents insight into their emotional development.

Real-world applications of emotional intelligence deserve special recognition. When sixteen-year-old Anthony used his conflict resolution skills to help mediate a dispute in his volunteer group, it showed how emotional competence translates into leadership abilities. These practical applications of emotional skills often indicate readiness for increased responsibility.

Remember that emotional growth isn't linear; there will be steps forward and occasional retreats. The key is maintaining a supportive presence while allowing natural consequences to serve as teachers. When seventeen-year-old Kerry struggled with time management during college applications, her initial stress led to better organization skills and increased self-advocacy - valuable tools for university life.

Decision-making milestones particularly deserve attention as they indicate growing emotional maturity. When fourteen-year-old Huw chose to distance himself from friends making risky choices, it demonstrated both emotional intelligence and the courage to act on his values. These moments of independent judgment show developing critical thinking skills essential for adult life.

Looking ahead, these emotional milestones lay the groundwork for future success. The self-awareness, resilience, and decision-making skills developed now become invaluable assets in college, careers, and relationships. As parents, our role is to recognize and reinforce this growth while maintaining appropriate expectations and support.

Most importantly, celebrating emotional growth isn't about perfection; it's about progress. Each step forward, whether managing disappointment better or showing increased empathy, contributes to the larger picture of emotional development. These skills become the foundation for lifelong learning, relationship building, and personal success in whatever path your child chooses to pursue. As we conclude this chapter on building resilience and fostering independence, let's reflect on the transformative journey of parenting with purpose and confidence. The roadmap we've explored isn't just about managing daily challenges; it's about equipping our children with the emotional intelligence, decision-making skills, and resilience they'll need throughout life's journey.

The stories we've shared, from Liza and her homework to Cameron's yard work, illustrate a fundamental truth: when we step back thoughtfully, our children step forward confidently. These moments of supported independence create more than just immediate solutions; they build the foundation for future success in relationships, careers, and personal growth. By implementing the Five-Step Resilience Building Framework and creating age-appropriate independence zones, we're not just solving today's challenges; we're investing in our children's lifelong capability to navigate their own path.

Perhaps most importantly, this approach to parenting helps develop critical thinking and problem-solving skills that extend far beyond childhood. When we allow natural consequences to teach within safe boundaries, we're preparing our children for the complex decisions they'll face in college, careers, and adult relationships. The confidence built through managing homework schedules or resolving peer conflicts becomes the foundation for tackling future challenges, whether choosing a career path or building professional relationships.

Remember that this journey isn't about perfection; it's about progress and growth for both parent and child. Each time you resist the urge to solve a problem your child can handle, you're building their resilience. Every moment you spend helping them process emotions rather than avoiding them strengthens their emotional intelligence. Your role isn't diminishing; it's evolving from primary problem-solver to trusted advisor and emotional coach.

As you move forward with these strategies, trust that the small steps of independence you're fostering today will lead to confident strides tomorrow. Whether your child is learning to pack their own lunch or making decisions about college, the principles remain the same: create safe spaces for growth, maintain emotional availability while stepping back, and celebrate the journey of becoming. Your child's path to independence may not always be smooth, but with your balanced support, it will be meaningful and empowering.

You have everything needed to implement these approaches effectively: the frameworks, the understanding, and most importantly, the deep commitment to your child's growth. Trust yourself, trust your child, and trust the process of building resilience through supported independence. The confidence you build in stepping back will echo through generations as your children learn to face life's challenges with resilience, wisdom, and unwavering self-trust.

Conclusion

As we conclude this journey together, I want to share a profound truth I've learned through decades of working with families: raising emotionally intelligent children isn't just about managing feelings; it's about nurturing future leaders, innovators, and compassionate adults who will shape tomorrow's world.

Think about Marco, the teenager I mentioned earlier, who struggled with decision-making because his parents had always chosen his classes and activities. When they finally stepped back, allowing him to select his own electives and extracurriculars, he initially felt overwhelmed. But through that experience, he discovered a passion for environmental science that later shaped his career path. Today, he credits those early opportunities to make independent choices with helping him develop the confidence to pursue his dreams.

Throughout this book, we've explored how trusting our children's journey extends far beyond emotional development. It's about cultivating critical thinking skills when we let them solve their own problems. It's about building resilience when we allow them to face and overcome challenges. It's about developing decision-making abilities when we step back and let them choose their path, even when it differs from what we might have chosen.

The tools and strategies we've discussed, from allowing natural consequences to creating safe spaces for emotional expression, are building blocks for life success. When children learn to manage their emotions independently, they develop the self-awareness needed for strong leadership. When they practice problem-solving without immediate parental intervention, they build the creativity and critical thinking skills essential for innovation. When they experience the results of their decisions, they develop the judgment needed for future career and life choices.

Consider how these skills translate into adulthood: The child who learns to regulate their emotions becomes the colleague who can handle workplace stress effectively. The teenager who develops independent decision-making skills becomes the professional who can confidently navigate career choices. The young person who builds resilience through overcoming challenges becomes the adult who can adapt to life's inevitable changes.

As you move forward, remember that every time you resist the urge to solve your child's problems, you're helping them develop the skills they'll need in college, in their careers, and their relationships. When you step back and let them manage age-appropriate tasks, you're preparing them for the independence they'll need in their professional lives. Each time you allow them to experience the natural consequences of their choices, you're helping them develop the judgment they'll need as adults.

Your role isn't to eliminate obstacles from your child's path; it's to equip them with the tools they need to overcome those obstacles themselves. This approach isn't just about raising happy children; it's about preparing capable, confident adults who can thrive in an increasingly complex world.

The journey doesn't end here. Each day brings new opportunities to apply these principles, to trust a little more, to step back a little further. And while the path may sometimes feel uncertain, remember that every step toward independence is a step toward your child's future success. You're not just raising a child; you're nurturing a future adult who will have the emotional intelligence, resilience, and decision-making skills to create their own path in life.

Trust their journey. Trust your guidance. Most importantly, trust that by allowing your child to develop these crucial life skills now, you're giving them the greatest gift possible: the ability to navigate their own way through life with confidence, competence, and emotional wisdom.

Bibliography

[1] YouNiverse Therapy. (2017, December 10). *8 Negative Effects of Overprotective Parenting*. YouNiverse Therapy. https://www.youniversetherapy.com/post/8-negative-effects-of-overprotective-parenting

[2] Arslan İ. B. (2023, January 12). *When Too Much Help is of No Help: Mothers' and Fathers' Perceived Overprotective Behavior and (Mal)Adaptive Functioning in Adolescents*. PMC - PubMed Central. https://pmc.ncbi.nlm.nih.gov/articles/PMC10027782/

[3] Meyers S. (2017, July 21). *The Root of Overprotective Parenting: Codependent Parents?*. Psychology Today. https://www.psychologytoday.com/us/blog/insight-is-2020/201707/the-root-overprotective-parenting-codependent-parents

[4] Arzt, N. (2023, November 8). *Overprotective Parents: Signs, Examples, & Effects on Mental Health*. Choosing Therapy. https://www.choosingtherapy.com/overprotective-parents/

[5] Waddle, J. (2019, August 20). *10 Signs Your Child Might Be Overprotected*. iBelieve. https://www.ibelieve.com/motherhood/10-signs-your-child-might-be-overprotected.html

[6] Hartley, E. (2024, September 19). *7 signs you were raised by well-meaning but overprotective parents*. Global English Editing.

https://geediting.com/signs-you-were-raised-by-well-meaning-but-overprotective-parents/

[7] Barth L. (2020, August 25). *Overprotective Parents: How to Let Go and Raise Independent Kids*. Healthline. https://www.healthline.com/health/parenting/overprotective-parents

[8] Noor S. (2024, November). *Overprotective Parents: Signs & Effects*. Faith Behavioral Health. https://faithbehavioralhealth.com/overprotective-parents/

[9] Salazar, D. (2019). *Book Review: Growing With: Every Parent's Guide to Helping Teenagers and Young Adults Thrive in Their Faith, Family, and Future by Kara Powell and Steven Argue*. Adventist Youth Ministries. https://adventistyouthministries.org/resources/book-reviews/book-review-growing-with-every-parent-s-guide-to-helping-teenagers-and-young-adults-thrive-in-their-faith-family-and-future-by-kara-powell-and-steven-argue

[10] Malik F., Marwaha R. (2022, September 18). *Developmental Stages of Social Emotional Development in Children*. StatPearls. https://www.ncbi.nlm.nih.gov/books/NBK534819/

[11] Help Me Grow Minnesota. (2023, December 01). *Social & Emotional Milestones*. Help Me Grow Minnesota. https://helpmegrowmn.org/HMG/DevelopMilestone/SocialEmotionalMilestones/index.html

[12] Meinke, H. (2019, December 30). *Understanding the Stages of Emotional Development in Children*. Rasmussen University. https://www.rasmussen.edu/degrees/education/blog/stages-of-emotional-development/

[13] Early Stages DC. (2023). *Social-Emotional Milestones*. Early Stages DC. https://www.earlystagesdc.org/page/social-emotional-milestones

[14] Sesame Workshop. (2024, January 01). *Emotional Milestones*. Sesame Workshop. https://sesameworkshop.org/resources/emotional-milestones/

[15] TerKeurst L. (2025, March). *The Trust Journey*. P31 Bookstore. https://www.p31bookstore.com/products/the-trust-journey

[16] Museo dei Bambini. (2024, August). *6 Parenting Books on Raising Healthy, Resilient Children*. Museo dei Bambini. https://www.museodeibambini.it/6-parenting-books-to-raising-healthy-resilient-children/

[17] Kaplan Early Learning Company. (2023, December 15). *Your Journey Together Resilience-Building Parenting Curriculum*. Kaplan Early Learning Company. https://www.kaplanco.com/product/74489/your-journey-together-resilience-building-parenting-curriculum?c=17%7CEA1000

[18] Bedortha, A., Davis, C., Swartz, L., & Thompson, J. (2020, August). *Natural versus Logical Consequences*. Parenting Now. https://parentingnow.org/natural-versus-logical-consequences/

[19] Suna, E. M. (2019, April 23). *Positive Parenting: Using Natural and Logical Consequences*. The Melissa Institute.

https://melissainstitute.org/positive-parenting-using-natural-and-logical-consequences/

[20] Lang, D. (2020). *Natural and Logical Consequences*. Parenting and Family Diversity Issues. https://iastate.pressbooks.pub/parentingfamilydiversity/chapter/natural-and-logical-consequences/

[21] Lee C. I. (2024, October 10). *Natural Consequences versus Logical Consequences*. La Concierge Psychologist. https://laconciergepsychologist.com/blog/natural-consequences-versus-logical-consequences/

[22] Bailey, B. (2018, November 27). *The Three Types of Consequences and How to Give Them*. Conscious Discipline. https://consciousdiscipline.com/three-types-of-consequences/

[23] TerKeurst L. (2024, December 10). *The Trust Journey: Heal from Broken Trust with Others, Yourself, and God (A Guided Journal to Use Alongside I Want to Trust You, but I Don't)*. FaithGateway. https://faithgateway.com/products/the-trust-journey-heal-from-broken-trust-with-others-yourself-and-god-a-guided-journal-to-use-alongside-i-want-to-trust-you-but-i-don-t-1

[24] Sanna, F. (2016, November 09). *Book Review: The Journey By Francesca Sanna*. Three Books a Night. https://threebooksanight.com/2016/11/09/the-journey-by-francesca-sanna/

25 Children's Trust Fund Alliance. (2024, February). *Book Club Guide for Parents*. Children's Trust Fund Alliance. https://ctfalliance.org/partnering-with-parents/book-club/

26 Our Little Play Nest. (2025, January 01). *Top 10 parenting books to read in 2025*. Our Little Play Nest. https://ourlittleplaynest.com/top-10-parenting-books-to-read-for-2025/

27 Bergman C. J. (2022, October 31). *Trust Kids!: Stories on Youth Autonomy and Confronting Adult Supremacy*. Goodreads. https://www.goodreads.com/book/show/60751223-trust-kids

28 Paris, J., Ricardo, A., & Rymond, D. (2019). *Child Growth and Development*. Palomar College Child Development Department. https://www.palomar.edu/childdevelopment/wp-content/uploads/sites/261/2020/07/CHDV-100-OER-Textbook-updatedJuly2020.pdf

29 Tot Play. (2015, April). *BookLook Review: Motivate Your Child*. Tot Play Blog. http://totplay.blogspot.com/2015/04/booklook-review-motivate-your-child.html

30 Seifert S. (2014, October 22). *How to Find Great Books to Read to Your Kids*. Focus on the Family. https://www.focusonthefamily.com/parenting/how-to-find-great-books-to-read-to-your-kids/

31 Dave. (2017, November 28). *Review: "Messy Journey" by Lori Wildenberg*. True Freedom Trust. https://truefreedomtrust.co.uk/review-messy-journey-lori-wildenberg

[32] Cherry K. (2024, May 02). *Erikson's Stages of Development.* Verywell Mind. https://www.verywellmind.com/erik-eriksons-stages-of-psychosocial-development-2795740

[33] Social Work Exam Strategies. (2024, January 01). *Trust Vs Mistrust: Early Childhood Development Stages.* Social Work Exams. https://socialworkexams.com/trust-vs-mistrust-early-childhood-development-stages/

[34] Suttie, J. (2008, September 1). *Life Stages of Trust.* Greater Good Magazine. https://greatergood.berkeley.edu/article/item/lifestagesof_trust

[35] McLeod S. (2008, April 18). *Erik Erikson's stages of psychosexual development.* Simply Psychology. https://www.simplypsychology.org/erik-erikson.html

[36] Powell K. & Argue S. (2019, March 4). *Growing With: Every Parent's Guide to Helping Teenagers and Young Adults Thrive in Their Faith, Family, and Future.* Goodreads. https://www.goodreads.com/en/book/show/40998407-growing-with

[37] SoBrief. (2024). *Top 5 Books on Parenting and Emotional Growth.* SoBrief. https://sobrief.com/lists/top-5-books-on-parenting-and-emotional-growth

[38] Koslowitz, R. (2025, July 01). *Post-Traumatic Parenting.* Broadleaf Books. https://www.broadleafbooks.com/store/product/9798889831174/Post-Traumatic-Parenting

[39] Flatley K. (2020, February). *14 of the Best Parenting Books to Raise Resilient, Successful, and Self-Sufficient Kids*. Self-Sufficient Kids. https://selfsufficientkids.com/best-parenting-books-raise-grounded-successful-kids/

[40] Michigan Kids Matter. (2023). *Social & Emotional Development Milestones for Toddlers (1 - 3 Years)*. Michigan.gov. https://www.michigan.gov/mikidsmatter/parents/toddler/social

[41] Esparza, R. (2023, November 8). *Emotional Development Milestones*. Ensemble Therapy. https://www.ensembletherapy.com/blog-posts/emotional-development-milestones

[42] Addiction Help. (2014, September). *The Six Developmental Stages of the Mind*. Addiction Help. http://addictionhelp.org/wp-content/uploads/2014/09/develop.pdf

Thank You for Reading!

I hope you found *Growing Confident and Capable Kids* helpful and enjoyable!

Your feedback is invaluable to me and helps others discover this book.

If you could take a moment to **leave a review**, I'd greatly appreciate it. Scan the QR code below to leave your review:

Thank you!

Patty

Visit the **Cantelune Press** website for more compassionate books that meet you where you are!

https://cantelunepress.com/

www.ingramcontent.com/pod-product-compliance
Lightning Source LLC
Chambersburg PA
CBHW061801120626
46550CB00005B/2087